GOING FISHING

A beginner's guide to
Freshwater Angling

GOING FISHING

A beginner's guide to Freshwater Angling

Tony Johnson

First edition - 2018

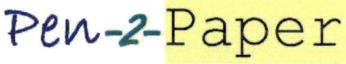

www.pen-2-paper.co.uk

Pen-2-Paper
86-90 Paul Street, London, EC2A 4NE
www.pen-2-paper.co.uk

ISBN: 9781723932700

First Edition Published 2018

Copyright © Pen-2-Paper 2018. All rights reserved.

The moral right of the author has been asserted.

No part of this publication may be reproduced, distributed or transmitted in any form or by any means, including printing, photocopying or other electronic or mechanical methods, without the prior written consent of the publisher, except as permitted under Copyright Law.

About the Author

Throughout his life, Tony Johnson has been fascinated by water and the fish within it. Every time he goes near a stream or pond, he has to look for the fish, to see if any are visible. On the few occasions he's rewarded with a glimpse of movement in the water, he immediately wonders what they're doing and what they're thinking.

It's that thought process that spawned a lifelong hobby – freshwater fishing. As a spotty teenager, barely 17 years old, Tony led a successful works match-angling team to several victories against other local organisations. The team, with their sights on success, fared well in the Angling Times Winter League, coming in at the top half of the league.

Tony has travelled extensively around the UK, in search of quality fish; not just big fish, but hard-to-reach fish, fighting fish, fish in unusual places, and the list goes on.

In this book, **Going Fishing: A Beginner's Guide to Freshwater Angling**, Tony shares his vast knowledge and experience of fishing, especially those early years spent learning the craft.

This book is intended as a guide and a reference to help beginners learn the ways of enjoying the wonderful pastime of freshwater fishing.

Preface

Fishing is a great leisure pursuit, enjoyed by millions around the world. By following the simple guidelines in this book, you can enjoy it too.

The book is mainly aimed at people, in the UK, who are keen to start freshwater (course) fishing, or maybe want to get better at it.

Use the book as a guide working from front to back, or as a reference book dipping into the relevant section using the contents or index.

However you use this book, I hope you enjoy it and learn something from it.

Acknowledgements

I believe I've learnt something from everyone I've ever fished with.

Even though I can't remember all the names, I thank you.

Credits

All photographs and illustrations © Caroline Lin

Except:

Sunset Angler (Front Cover and Page ii)	ID 45723790 © Mikhail Dudarev | Dreamstime.com
Little Boy (Page viii)	ID 55891907 © Grafvision | Dreamstime.com
Floats Bunch (Page 6)	ID 5755102 © Igor Golovniov | Dreamstime.com
Plug (Page 22)	ID 116332031 © Publicdomainphotos | Dreamstime.com
Rod actions (Page 28)	ID 80508292 © Anton Novik | Dreamstime.com
Knots Chart (Page 55)	ID 23554435 © Boris Kondrashov | Dreamstime.com
Floats (Page 76)	ID 77536003 © Smiltena | Dreamstime.com
Rod Bend (Page 102)	ID 11230744 © Charles Dyer | Dreamstime.com

Thanks to Suffolk Water Park for permission to publish the photographs on Pages 2, 4, 64 and 97.

Dedications

Special thanks to my parents, my brother, and my sister; each inspires me in a unique way.

List of Charts, Illustrations and Photographs

Chart One – What to catch	18
Chart Two – How to catch	19
Chart Three – What hookbait to use	20
Chart Four – Knots	55
Illustration One – Rod actions	28
Illustration Two – Fishing rod	29
Illustration Three – Fixed spool reel	30
Illustration Four – Hook	38
Illustration Five – Rod rest	43
Illustration Six – Figure of Eight knot	56
Illustration Seven – Grinner knot	57
Illustration Eight – Half Blood knot	58
Illustration Nine – Palomar knot	59
Illustration Ten – Canal cross-section	62
Illustration Eleven – Lure Casting pattern	74
Illustration Twelve – Dropshot rig	75
Illustration Thirteen – Stillwater setup	87
Illustration Fourteen – Feeder rig	86
Illustration Fifteen – Plumbing	88
Illustration Sixteen – Shot patterns – Stillwaters	90
Illustration Seventeen – Shot patterns – Rivers	92
Illustration Eighteen – Casting	95
Photo One – Sunset angler	Front Cover, ii
Photo Two – Little boy	viii
Photo Three – Drain	x
Photo Four – Large lake	2
Photo Five – Small lake	4
Photo Six – Floats bunch	6
Photo Seven – Bleak	8
Photo Eight – Gudgeon	8
Photo Nine – Ruffe	9
Photo Ten – Dace	9

Photo Eleven – Silver Bream	10
Photo Twelve – Grayling	10
Photo Thirteen – Roach	11
Photo Fourteen – Crucian Carp	11
Photo Fifteen – Rudd	12
Photo Sixteen – Perch	12
Photo Seventeen – Chub	13
Photo Eighteen – Eel	13
Photo Nineteen – Tench	14
Photo Twenty – Bream	14
Photo Twenty-one – Barbel	15
Photo Twenty-two – Zander	15
Photo Twenty-three – Pike	16
Photo Twenty-four – Wels Catfish	16
Photo Twenty-five – Carp	17
Photo Twenty-six – Plug	22
Photo Twenty-seven – Cage Feeder	37
Photo Twenty-eight – Maggot feeder	37
Photo Twenty-nine – Method feeder	37
Photo Thirty – Hooks	38
Photo Thirty-one – Disgorgers	39
Photo Thirty-two – Plummets	39
Photo Thirty-three – Float stops	40
Photo Thirty-four – Maggots	46
Photo Thirty-five – Casters	47
Photo Thirty-six – Worms	47
Photo Thirty-seven – Sweetcorn	50
Photo Thirty-eight – Pellets	50
Photo Thirty-nine – Boilies	52
Photo Forty – Artificial hookbaits	52
Photo Forty-one – Pole fishing	60
Photo Forty-two – Canal	63
Photo Forty-three – Lake	64
Photo Forty-four – Slow-moving river	66
Photo Forty-five – Fast-moving river	68
Photo Forty-six – Drain	69
Photo Forty-seven – Floats	76
Photo Forty-eight – Canal fishing	80
Photo Forty-nine – Aim at a target	97
Photo Fifty – Rod Bend	102

Table of Contents

About the Author — i

Preface — ii

Acknowledgements — iii

Dedications — iv

Lists of Charts, Illustrations and Photographs — v

How to use this book — ix

Introduction — 1

ONE — A Brief History of Fishing — 3

TWO — Where are you going to fish? — 5

THREE — Equipment — 23

FOUR — Where to fish and the methods to use — 61

FIVE — Specialist fishing — 71

SIX — It's time to go fishing — 77

SEVEN — Going Fishing — 81

Annex One — 107

Annex Two — 111

Annex Three — 113

Annex Four — 115

Terminology — 117

Index — 133

How to use this book

Going Fishing guides the reader through the often confusing choices they need to make as they're beginning a new pastime – freshwater fishing.

The book provides a logical step-by-step approach to deciding where to fish and what equipment, method and bait to use.

It then goes on to explain how to set up the equipment and approach the water. With clear descriptions and illustrations, the different types of fish, waters and methods are described in detail. The book is intended as a guide and a reference to help the beginner catch fish.

Throughout the book, I provide particularly important INFORMATION, which is indicated by the symbol - . Please don't ignore this information.

I give useful ADVICE on particular aspects of freshwater fishing, which is accompanied by the symbol -

Within the book, I've also included TOP TIPS and QUOTATIONS.

A short note on terminology, like every pastime, anglers have their own language. At the end of this book, I've included a list of the most common terms and an index of topics.

Introduction

Freshwater angling, or coarse fishing as it's sometimes called, is one of the UK's most popular pastimes. It appeals to all people, despite their age, ability or income. On average, over 100,000 people go freshwater fishing every week in the UK.

I got into fishing when I was maybe 12 or 13 years old. I merely went fishing with a friend, and I was instantly hooked. Using light tackle to catch fish in a slow-moving river entirely enthralled me; the anticipation of the bite, the catch, and getting fish onto the bank – it was magic. Within months, with lots of practice and many mistakes, I became a far better angler than my friend – I was catching, and he wasn't; I haven't seen him since.

Starting any new pastime or sport is often daunting; there's a lot to learn – the techniques, the equipment, the terminology, and so on. At the outset, freshwater fishing can be challenging for the beginner; there are so many types of fish, baits, lines, hooks, floats, etc. where should we start?

Let's start by explaining the terms used to describe the pastime of fishing. There are three basic types of angling: sea, game and course. Sea anglers catch sea fish (not with a net), game anglers catch salmon, trout and char, and course anglers catch the freshwater fish that are not game fish. I hope this explanation clears some of the confusion. Generally, people who fish are called anglers, but they do not go angling – they go fishing. There, clear as mud.

It's easy for anyone to make mistakes in the early days and end-up buying equipment which isn't suitable (every angler has equipment they never use), to damage the tackle in use, or to come away from your favourite fishing spot without catching a fish.

Don't worry, by the end of the book you'll have the right gear and be on your way to being a great angler.

GOING FISHING

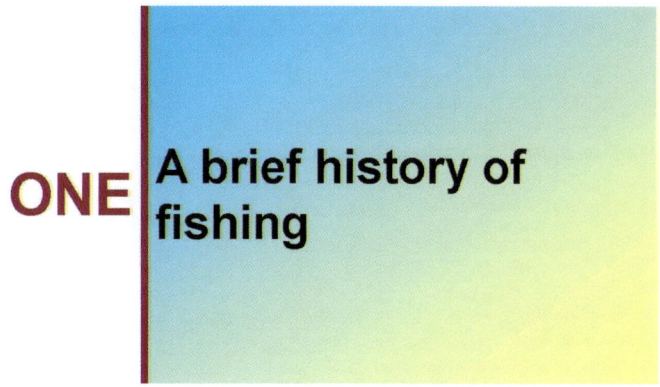

ONE: A brief history of fishing

The practice of catching fish with a hook and line dates back about twenty thousand years; stone age people caught fish to eat.

Possibly the first and most famous book on pleasure fishing *The Compleat Angler*, by Isaac Walton, was published in 1653. The book confesses to being a 'celebration of the art and spirit of fishing'. The book heralded the rising prominence of a new pastime.

Early fishing equipment was made from natural materials such as cane and bamboo, as such it was cumbersome and expensive, and often required extensive care and maintenance. Whereas modern equipment is advanced, lightweight, and easily maintained.

Angling gained enormous popularity as a sport in the 1950s onwards. Fishing competitions were held locally, regionally, nationally and internationally. Match fishing, a form of angling where people fish for a defined period to catch the most fish (by weight), helped bolster the number of anglers engaged in the hobby and sport. After a brief decline in popularity, freshwater fishing is more popular than ever.

Course anglers don't take their catch home; gone are the days when people fished for food; Anglers always return their catch to the water.

> The number of anglers in the UK has increased by around 1.2 million (that's almost 20%) in the past ten years.

GOING FISHING

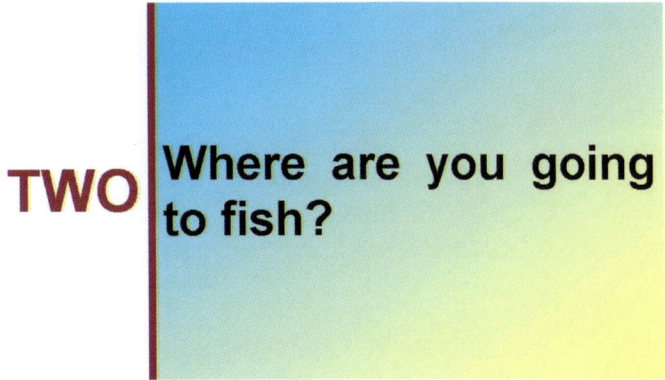

TWO — Where are you going to fish?

Do you know, this is possibly the most relevant question to ask an angler as they're starting? Where are you going to fish?

The answer to the question determines what fish might be caught, what tackle and equipment might be needed, what licences and permits will be required, and lots of other important stuff.

Anyone new to angling is not going to book an expensive two-week vacation on a big carp fishery in Ukraine, so let's assume you will fish somewhere easily accessible.

It makes sense to choose a fishing spot close to your home; maybe somewhere you're familiar with. Since you're just starting, it might be best to avoid places:

That are busy with runners, walkers, cyclists, etc.

With lots of vegetation and obstacles around them

On a steep slope

With overhead powerlines

With lots of boat traffic

On a narrow bank, such as some canal towpaths.

 ADVICE:

As you're deciding where to fish, choose a place where you can watch other anglers and learn from them. Once you've decided where to fish, I would advise you to fish in the same place until you feel confident.

DO NOT keep trying new places until you've built your confidence and ability to confront a range of waters.

> One of the best ways to learn is to watch others. Look how other anglers fish; observe the tackle, methods and baits they're using. You'll soon discover what works, and what doesn't.

Make it easy for yourself, find a flat spot with lots of open space around and with no fear of someone tripping over (and breaking) your tackle.

As with any new pastime, small mistakes can be expected from the outset, so it's best to avoid places which present a challenge.

In my early days as an angler, I fished Lake Burwain, a canal-feeding reservoir with gently-sloping muddy banks into shallow water (I won a match there aged 16); I also fished the Leeds and Liverpool Canal and won several matches over many years.

From the age of 14, I simply learned the art of fishing on those two contrasting waters and got good at it. As soon as I could drive, I had the skills and knowledge to venture further afield.

WHERE ARE YOU GOING TO FISH?

Types of water and what fish might be in them

Freshwater fish live in either still water or flowing water.

Stillwaters include reservoirs/lakes, ponds, and canals.

Flowing waters include rivers, streams and drains.

IMPORTANT:

The Law says that you cannot fish for coarse fish on rivers, streams or drains between 15 March and 15 June (the close season).

The ban on fishing during the close season allows fish to spawn.

Some stillwaters and canals also impose restrictions on fishing during the close season.

Local bylaws impose restrictions on fishing for eels during the close season.

Local bylaws also impose different close seasons for game fishing.

Check the local bylaws.

Some fish live in both still and flowing water, depending on the speed of the flow. The following pages contain a comprehensive guide to where the fish live and how we might catch them.

In the guide we include the common freshwater fish to be found in the UK, starting with the smallest (bleak and gudgeon) and gradually moving towards the largest (carp).

In this section we introduce terms that might be unfamiliar; don't worry – you can check the terminology at the back of the book.

The details, such as hook sizes, bait types, and methods of fishing, will be explained later.

Bleak

Bleak (a small silver elongated fish) can be found in slow-moving or still waters.

They move in shoals feeding in the upper layers of the water. Bleak are often mistaken, due to their small size, for the young of other fish such as roach.

Bleak grow to about 4oz (0.25lb) in the UK.

Bleak are usually caught using light fishing tackle: typically using a float, 1lb line and a size 22 hook.

Maggots, casters, small worms, and bread are the favoured baits.

Gudgeon

Gudgeon (a small elongated brown-spotted fish) can be found in fast-moving rivers.

They feed on the gravelly or stony bed. Gudgeon are often mistaken, due to their similar appearance, for young barbel. Gudgeon grow to about 5oz in the UK.

Gudgeon are usually caught using light fishing tackle: typically using a float, 1lb line and a size 22 hook.

Maggots, casters, small worms, and bread are the favoured baits.

Ruffe

Ruffe (a small pale brown fish with a spiny dorsal fin) can be found in slow-moving or still waters.

They move in shoals feeding from the bed of the lake or river. Ruffe is often mistaken, due to their similar appearance, for young perch. Ruffe grows to about 5oz in the UK.

Ruffe is usually caught using light fishing tackle: typically using a float, 1lb line and a size 20/22 hook.

Maggots, and small worms, and chopped worm are the favoured baits.

Dace

Dace (a slender, fast silver and red fish) can be found in fast flowing water around weirs.

They often move in shoals around the middle and upper layers of the water. Dace grow to just over 1lb in the UK.

Dace is usually caught using light fishing tackle: typically using a float, 1lb line, and a size 20 hook. Dace are very wary, so the tackle must be as light as possible.

Maggots, casters, small worms, and bread are the favoured baits, due to the small mouth of the dace.

Silver Bream

Silver Bream (a deep bodied silver fish with a dark green back) can be found in slowing moving and still waters. They move in shoals feeding in the lower layers of water. Silver bream are frequently mistaken for young bream – often a scale count is the only method of identification. Silver Bream grow to just over 2lb in the UK.

They are usually caught across a range of methods:

Float, 1½lb line and a size 18 hook

Leger, 1½lb line and a size 18 hook

Feeder, 1½lb line and a size 18 hook.

Maggots, casters, small worms, and bread are the favoured baits.

Grayling

Grayling (a streamlined silver fish with a large dorsal fin) can be found in fast flowing rivers and streams that are clean and well-oxygenated. They often move in shoals through all the layers of the water, feeding on the bottom and taking flies from the surface. Grayling grow to just over 4lb in the UK.

They are usually caught across a range of methods:

Float, 2lb line and a size 18 hook

Leger, 2lb line and a size 18 hook

Feeder, 2lb line and a size 18 hook.

Maggots, casters, small worms, and bread are the favoured baits.

Roach

Roach (a deep bodied silver fish with a dark back and red lower fins) can be found in stillwaters, canals and slow-moving rivers. They move in shoals feeding on the bottom. Roach grow to just over 4lb in the UK.

They are usually caught across a range of methods:

Float, 2lb line and a size 18 hook

Leger, 2lb line and a size 18 hook

Feeder, 2lb line and a size 18 hook.

Maggots, casters, small worms, hempseed, and bread are the favoured baits.

Crucian Carp

Crucian Carp (a deep round bodied bronze fish with red fins – a member of the carp family) can be mainly found in stillwaters. They move in shoals around all layers of the water, feeding on the bottom and taking insects from the surface. Crucians grow to just over 4½lb in the UK.

They are usually caught across a range of methods:

Float, 2lb line and a size 18 hook

Leger, 2lb line and a size 18 hook

Feeder, 2lb line and a size 18 hook.

Maggots, casters, small worms, sweetcorn, and bread are the favoured baits.

Rudd

Rudd (a deep bodied golden fish with a dark back and red lower fins) can be found in overgrown stillwaters, canals, and slow-moving rivers.

They move in shoals feeding from the lower layer of water. Rudd grows to just over 4½lb in the UK.

They are usually caught across a range of methods:

Float, 2lb line and a size 18 hook

Leger, 2lb line and a size 18 hook

Feeder, 2lb line and a size 18 hook.

Maggots, casters, small worms, and bread are the favoured baits.

Perch

Perch (a flat-sided green fish with black stripes and spiny dorsal fins) can be found in almost all types of freshwater, usually close to underwater obstacles, structures, tree roots, etc. Perch grow to almost 5lb in the UK.

They are usually caught across a range of methods:

Float, 3lb line and a size 16 hook

Leger, 3lb line and a size 16 hook

Feeder, 3lb line and a size 16 hook

Spinner, 4lb line with a small plug, lure or spinner.

Maggots, casters, worms, small fish, and bread are the favoured baits.

Chub

Chub (a cylindrical green fish with red fins) can be found in fast flowing water around weirs, or in rivers and streams that are clean and well-oxygenated, and in stillwaters. Smaller fish often move in shoals around the middle layers of the water. Chub grow to over 9lb in the UK.

They are usually caught across a range of methods:

Float, 4lb line and a size 16-10 hook

Leger, 4lb line and a size 16-10 hook

Feeder, 4lb line and a size 16-10 hook

Maggots, casters, worms, small fish (deadbaits), sweetcorn, slugs, cheese, shrimps, berries, boilies, and bread (just about everything) are the favoured baits. Chub are even caught with lures.

Eel

Eels (a snake-like fish with a colour variation from silver to black) can be found in almost all types of freshwater, usually close to underwater obstacles. Eels feed on the bottom. Eels grow to over 11lb in the UK.

They are usually caught across a range of methods:

Float, 4lb line and a size 16/14 hook

Leger, 4lb line and a size 16/14 hook

Feeder, 4lb line and a size 16/14 hook

Maggots, casters, worms, and small fish (deadbaits) are the favoured baits.

Tench

Tench (a rounded olive coloured fish with rounded fins) can be found in canals, stillwaters and slow-moving rivers. They move in shoals feeding on the bottom by rooting around in the mud.

Tench grow to just over 15lb in the UK.

They are usually caught across a range of methods:

Float, 5lb line and a size 14 hook

Leger, 5lb line and a size 14 hook

Feeder, 5lb line and a size 14 hook.

Maggots, casters, worms, sweetcorn, small boilies, and bread are the favoured baits.

Bream

Bream (a deep bodied slimy bronze fish) can be mainly found in canals, stillwaters and slow-moving rivers. They often move in large shoals feeding on the bottom by rooting around in the mud. Bream grow to almost 20lb in the UK.

They are usually caught across a range of methods:

Float, 4lb line and a size 16 hook

Leger, 4lb line and a size 16 hook

Feeder, 4lb line and a size 16 hook.

Maggots, casters, worms, sweetcorn, and bread are the favoured baits.

Barbel

Barbel (a brown cylindrical fish with barbules either size of its thick lips) can be found in fast moving waters feeding on the bottom. Barbel grow up to over 21lb in the UK.

They are usually caught across a range of methods:

Float, 6-8lb line and a size 12-8 hook

Leger, 6-8lb line and a size 12-8 hook

Feeder, 6-8lb line and a size 12-8 hook.

Maggots, casters, worms (large and small), sweetcorn, meat, cheese, boilies and bread are the favoured baits.

Zander

Zander (a grey-brown fish with vague stripes, sharp fangs and a spiny dorsal fin) can be found in stillwaters and slow-moving rivers. Zander grow to over 21lb in the UK.

They are usually caught across a range of methods:

Float, 15lb line and a size 10-4 treble hook

Leger, 15lb line and a size 10-4 treble hook

Spinner, 20lb line with a plug, lure or spinner.

Small freshwater fish (dead or alive) are the favoured baits.

Pike

Pike (a long green cylindrical fish with a patterned body and large mouth with sharp teeth) can be mainly found in canals, stillwaters and slow-moving rivers. Pike will eat anything that it moves in or around the water.

Pike grow to over 46lb in the UK.

They are usually caught across a range of methods:

Float, 20-30lb line and a size 10-4 treble hook

Leger, 20-30lb line and a size 10-4 treble hook

Spinner, 25-35lb line with a plug, lure or spinner.

Small freshwater fish (dead or alive) are the favoured baits.

Wels Catfish

Wels Catfish (a long dark scale-less fish with a big mouth and long barbules) can be mainly found in stillwaters. Catfish patrol the water looking for anything (dead or alive) to eat.

Wels Catfish grow to over 60lb in the UK.

They are usually caught using:

Float, 20-30lb braided line and a size 10-4 treble hook

Leger, 20-30lb braided line and a size 10-4 treble hook

Small freshwater fish (dead or alive) are the favoured baits.

Carp

Carp (a diverse family of fish, each with a distinctive scale pattern) can be found in one form or another in most stillwaters and slow-moving rivers. Carp often feed in shoals by grubbing across the bottom.

Consequently, heavy groundbaiting is often required to attract the fish to your 'swim'. Carp grow up to almost 70lb in the UK.

They are usually caught across a range of methods:

Float, 8-10lb line and a size 12-4 hook

Leger, 8-10lb line and a size 12-4 hook

Feeder, 8-10lb line and a size 12-4 hook.

Maggots, casters, large worms, sweetcorn, meat, cheese, boilies and bread are the favoured baits.

Chart One – What to catch

Let's have a look at Chart One to see what you might find at your chosen spot. The best ways to discover what fish could be caught is to ask other anglers, to watch other anglers, or to ask the local fishing tackle shop.

	Canal	Lake	River	Drain
Bleak		x	Slow	
Gudgeon			Fast	
Ruffe		x	Slow	x
Dace			Fast	
Silver Bream	x	x	Slow	
Grayling			Fast	
Roach	x	x	Slow	x
Crucian Carp	x	x		
Rudd	x	x	Slow	
Perch	x	x	Slow	x
Chub		x	Slow & Fast	x
Eel		x	Slow	x
Tench	x	x	Slow	
Bream	x	x	Slow	x
Barbel			Slow & Fast	
Zander	x	x	Slow	x
Pike	x	x	Slow	x
Wels Catfish			Slow	x
Carp	x	x	Slow	

Chart Two – How to catch

Chart Two indicates what methods might be used to catch each type of fish. Again, the best ways to discover what methods should be used is to ask other anglers, to watch other anglers, or to ask the local fishing tackle shop.

	Float	Leger/Feeder	Lure	Line	Hook
Bleak	x			1lb	22
Gudgeon	x			1lb	22
Ruffe	x			1lb	22
Dace	x			1lb	20
Silver Bream	x	x		1½lb	18
Grayling	x	x		2lb	18
Roach	x	x		2lb	16
Crucian Carp	x	x		2lb	16
Rudd	x	x		2lb	16
Perch	x	x	x	3-4lb	16
Chub	x	x	x	4-6lb	14
Eel	x	x		4lb	14
Tench	x	x		5lb	14
Bream	x	x		5lb	14
Barbel	x	x		6-8lb	12
Zander	x	x	x	15-20lb	10
Pike	x	x	x	20-35lb	10
Wels Catfish	x	x		20-30lb	8
Carp	x	x		10-20lb	8

Chart Three – What hookbait to use

Chart Three details the hookbaits which could be used to catch each type of fish. Again, the best ways to discover what baits should be used is to ask other anglers, to watch other anglers, or to ask the local fishing tackle shop.

	Maggot	Bread	Corn	Boilies	Deadbaits
Bleak	x	x			
Gudgeon	x				
Ruffe	x				
Dace	x	x			
Silver Bream	x	x	x		
Grayling	x	x			
Roach	x	x	x		
Crucian Carp	x	x	x		
Rudd	x	x	x		
Perch	x				x
Chub	x	x	x		x
Eel	x				x
Tench	x	x	x	x	
Bream	x	x	x	x	
Barbel	x	x	x	x	
Zander					x
Pike					x
Wels Catfish					x
Carp	x	x	x	x	

The type of water and the fish to be caught determine the fishing methods, which dictates the tackle and bait.

You're not, for example, going to catch any roach (silver fish) with tackle suited to catching pike (predator with teeth), and vice versa. Carefully choose where you will fish; your investment in fishing equipment will be based on that decision.

The weight of the fish you want to catch also plays a significant part in deciding where to fish, as does the time you want to devote to the pastime.

Do you want to catch a dozen 8 to 12oz roach in an afternoon session or one 40lb carp on a week-long trip? The latter is probably unrealistic for a beginner.

However, it's for you to decide. Have you chosen a place to fish? Do you know what fish you might catch?

If so, let's move on.

 **IMPORTANT:**

Fish don't always obey the 'rules' on where they should live or what they should eat.

Use the information presented here as a guide.

GOING FISHING

PAGE 22

THREE | Equipment

Step into any fishing tackle shop or open any tackle catalogue and you're faced with a massive array of specialist equipment, which gives the angler a wide choice but can be bewildering for beginners. When starting, you need the tackle and equipment which can be used for a range of fishing methods. So, I suggest you avoid specialist equipment for now.

In this section, we detail each piece of equipment you need to catch fish. Some are essential, and some are preferential – let's take a look.

Licence and permit

Although they're not equipment, you're not going to do any fishing without a Rod Licence and a fishing permit.

Some people get confused between the two; it's simple, the licence allows you to fish (like a driving licence), and the permit allows you to fish in a particular place (like a car park ticket).

Make sure you have a licence and a permit before you start fishing, or you could be fined up to £2,500.

I IMPORTANT:

You must carry your licence at all times when fishing.

GOING FISHING

The good news is children under 13 don't need a licence, but people between 13 and 16 do need a licence, and it's free.

Check local bylaws, as local variations may apply, such as on the River Thames.

The licence you need for coarse fishing is called a *Trout, coarse fish and eel licence*, which allows 2 rods to be used (by the same person) for coarse fishing.

You can buy a licence for 1-day, 8-days or 12-months. The licence can be purchased online (www.gov.uk/fishing-licences) or at a Post Office; avoid using other online outlets to obtain your licence – some charge a fee.

Permits are often more complicated; you must check how to purchase your permit BEFORE fishing. Some are available on the bank, in which case you can fish, and pay the warden when they collect payment. Sometimes only 12-month permits are available; these are often classed as memberships which require an angler to apply for the membership before fishing.

Be sure you know the permit rules BEFORE you fish - don't get charged with trespassing. Again, for advice, ask the local tackle shop – they often sell permits and memberships for local waters and clubs.

You should read the permit carefully, as it will detail any restrictions on baits to be used, ground-baiting, and the use of nets, as well as other valuable information. If in doubt, ask the person who sold you the permit.

Many commercial fisheries sell Day Tickets allowing anglers to pay for one day. Overnight fishing may be available, but this often has to be pre-booked, especially on waters holding big carp.

Annexes Two and Three contain typical and interesting rules you might find on your permit.

I IMPORTANT:

Follow the rules specified in the permit.

Do not assume that all fisheries specify the same rules.

Clothing

Again, it's not equipment, but apparel plays an essential role in your fishing experience. It must be comfortable, waterproof, durable, warm (on cold days), cool (on hot days), and allow you to move freely.

You will have clothing preferences, so I will not list all the options.

I always wear layers of clothing so I can remove a layer if I get too warm. My outer clothing is durable and easily washable, my footwear is a pair of hiking boots. However, depending on the bank of the river, canal or lake, it might be useful to consider wellington boots, or something similar.

If you're visiting the fishing venue before you fish, you can determine the best footwear.

Many anglers wear a cap to shield their eyes and face from the sun; it's a personal choice that's worth considering.

Food and drink

Again, it's not equipment, but it is vitally important that you eat and drink while you're fishing.

There are many practical considerations when choosing what food to take on your fishing trip. First, you must pick food that will not perish in the heat. Second, you must select food that will not be contaminated by your dirty fingers (covered in fish slime, maggot juice, groundbait, and so on). I would avoid chicken drumsticks, or cucumber sandwiches, and choose something that's packaged. Typical foods on my list include crisps, Pepperami (other brands are available), and bananas. All can be eaten directly from the pack without touching them (HINT: you must crush the crisps in the bag first).

For long fishing trips, it's also important to consider different types of food – fruit, vegetables, protein, carbs, etc.

You could carry wet wipes to clean your hands, in which case you can touch the food – this opens the range of options (to include cucumber sandwiches).

I always choose cold drinks and carry a few screw-top plastic bottles. I'm aware of the eco-pressure on not using plastic, but it's convenient and much safer than glass. I sometimes carry a flask of hot tea in winter to keep me warm.

Seat

Depending on your chosen method of fishing, and the tackle you will use, you probably need to sit. I haven't seen many pole anglers standing while fishing (more on using a pole later).

Maybe it's just me, but I like to be comfortable when I'm fishing, so my seat is important. It also doubles as a massive tackle box, with lots of little drawers, trays, and sticks for me to add rod/pole rests, and so on. Choose a seat you can afford but one which is comfortable. My first fishing seat was a folding picnic chair; it was cumbersome to carry, but it worked until I could afford something better. I've had my seat box for about 15 years, and it is still the best piece of equipment I ever bought.

Shelter

Consider what might happen if it starts to rain or blow a gale, while you're fishing. One of the first pieces of kit I bought was a second-hand fishing umbrella; living in the north, it was essential equipment. The investment paid dividends within weeks – it seemed to rain every time I went fishing. Simply, I wouldn't have been able to fish without that brolly.

If rain could possibly spoil your fun, think about investing in a brolly.

I IMPORTANT:

Umbrellas make great shelters but can also make good kites. Make sure the umbrella is firmly anchored to stop it blowing away.

EQUIPMENT

I recall Boxing Day 1977; I'd received a new brolly as a Christmas present from my parents. I sat on the bank of Lake Burwain in a torrential downpour, trying to find the elusive shoals of bream. It wasn't windy as I sat proudly under my new shelter . . . until a gust suddenly hit. The first I knew was the umbrella pivoting forward at speed, hitting my rod, tumbling once and taking off across the lake. Another lesson learnt; anchor the brolly in future.

As I watched the brolly slowing sinking about 20 yards out, I knew what I had to do. I quickly packed my tackle away, ready for a hasty departure. Then, without hesitation, I waded into the lake to retrieve my new shelter (at low water, Lake Burwain is shallow, so I knew I was safe).

I IMPORTANT:

Never wade into water unless it is necessary, and you know how deep it is (and it's not freezing, as it was on Boxing Day 1977).

Tackle

Fishing tackle is a collective term for the equipment that an angler needs to catch fish. Primarily, the equipment includes a rod or pole, reel, line, floats, weights, and hooks. There's a plethora of other gear that's needed, such as nets, bait boxes, rod rests, and disgorgers. Over these pages, let's go through all this stuff, and offer guidance on what tackle you need.

As you're a beginner to this wonderful pastime, I would suggest that you avoid specialist or specimen fishing to start with. However, it is entirely your choice, so I'll cover some of the specialist tackle and methods separately in the next chapter.

Let's go back to Chart One, showing what fish are typically found where. I hope you have seen your chosen water type (canal, lake, river, or drain) in the chart. Likewise, I hope you found the fish to be caught in the chart and, typically, they are (highlighted in blue) silver bream, grayling, roach, crucian carp, rudd, perch, chub, eel, tench, and bream.

GOING FISHING

Chart Two shows the methods that might be used with those same fish (highlighted in blue) and, typically, they are a float, leger and feeder. Perch and chub might also be caught using a spinner or lure, so let's include spinning in the next chapter too.

Rod

By homing in on the waters to be fished and the fish to be caught, we've identified three conventional methods to catch most fish: float, leger and feeder. A typical float rod would be between 11ft and 14ft long, comprising three sections of equal length.

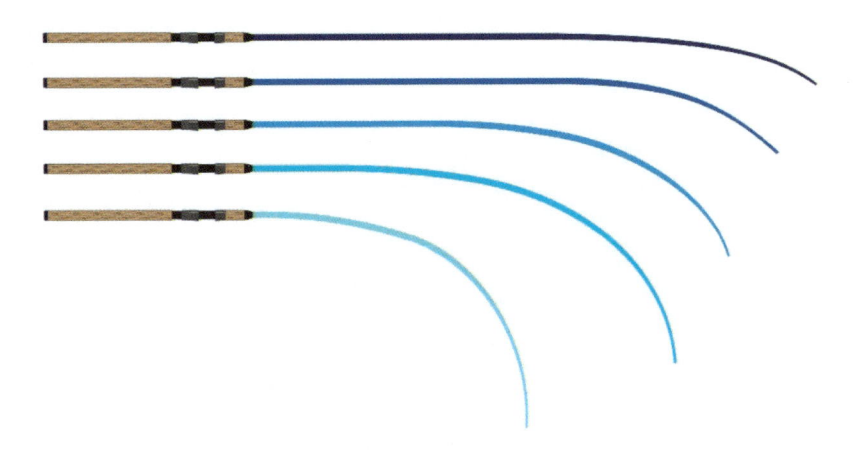

For a beginner, the action of the rod isn't vitally important – unless the price isn't a problem. Choose a rod for match fishing at a price that's affordable.

There are different types of action for float rods from 'tip action' to 'through action' which describes where the maximum bend occurs.

For general fishing go for something in between 'tip' and 'through' action. 'Tip action' is where the bend occurs in the section nearest the tip of the rod, 'through action' is where the bend occurs through the entire rod.

Leger and feeder rods are basically the same, as is the fishing method. Leger/feeder rods are generally around 11ft to 12ft.

For all-round flexibility, I would recommend purchasing a Match Rod of between 11ft and 13ft; this should provide all the features of the float rod and leger/feeder rod. Try to get one with a screw fitting on the tip ring to accommodate a quiver tip.

All fishing rods require a reel to hold the line, to cast the hookbait, and to control the fish.

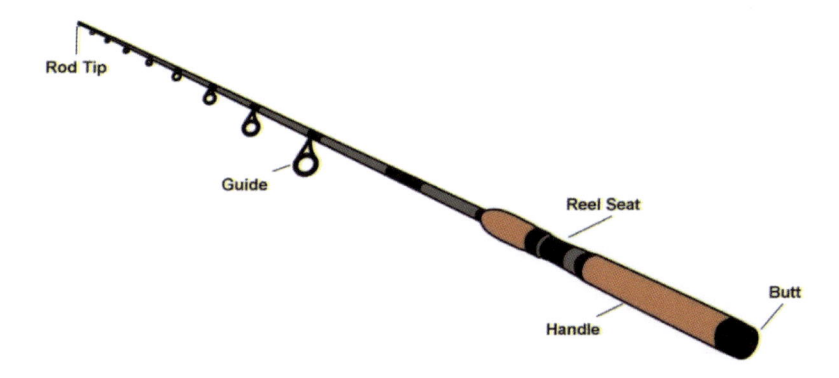

Feeder rods often include more than one tip section; each with different stiffness. The different sections provide the ability for the angler to approach a range of fish on various types of water.

Pole

For precision float fishing, the pole is a formidable piece of equipment. Poles require no reel since the line is attached directly to the pole, usually using a cone fitment inside the pole sections with an elastic shock absorber between the pole and the line.

Pole fishing is often the chosen method for match anglers, and it allows hookbait presentation in precisely the same place every time.

Pole floats are much lighter than floats used with rods. There is a limitation on how far the float can be cast; this is dictated by the length of the pole combined with the line length and the float depth. A 16ft pole will not be able to fish 60 feet out; it will probably be limited to around 20ft.

Poles are measured in metres, not in feet like rods; aim for an 8m to 10m pole with a medium action and an elastic rating of around 8. Such an elastic will provide good all-round flexibility and be able to cope with more substantial, hard-fighting fish.

Fishing a pole requires intense concentration, the pole must be handled continuously, which can be tiring at first as the top section must be disconnected and reconnected repeatedly, and the entire pole has to be shipped backwards and forwards. Unlike a fishing rod, a pole can't just be placed in a rod rest - it's usually too heavy. Instead, it must be balanced comfortably across the lap of the angler.

Pole fishing often requires a pole roller; a device that allows the pole to run across it without causing damage. The roller is usually placed 10-12ft behind the angler, and they put the pole into it as they retrieve the hookbait or play the fish.

If the prospect of using a pole sounds slightly daunting, why not choose a shorter pole initially, perhaps a telescopic pole which could be mastered within minutes? A 5m whip (short telescopic pole) is inexpensive and a great way to catch smaller fish.

> When fishing a pole, sit sideways and place the pole across your upper thighs. Rest your forearm across the top of the pole, and your other hand under the pole in front of you.

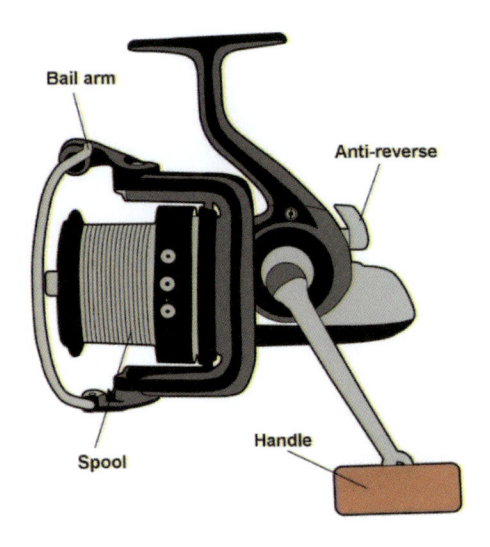

Reel

For course fishing, there are two basic reels: centrepin and fixed spool. The centrepin is often used to trot a float down a river (it maintains good contact with the float); whereas, the fixed-spool reel is used for all types of fishing.

Centrepin reels don't allow long casts, the movement is underarm and aims to flick the float into the water smoothly. The beauty of such a reel is the constant feeding of the line which means the rod is always in contact with the float as it goes with the flow. A centrepin reel is essential for anglers who want to trot a float down a river with the current.

EQUIPMENT

For a beginner, I would strongly recommend a fixed-spool reel as it's easy to master and, generally, helps avoid tangled line (although there will be one or two mishaps initially).

A fixed spool reel works by winding the line around a fixed spool using an armature or bail arm. The face of the spool faces forward, and that's where the line goes in the cast.

The cast is simple, trap the line against the rod handle with your finger to prevent the line dropping of the spool, disengage the bail arm, and cast the hookbait towards the water releasing the line to get greater distance in the cast. Re-engage the bail arm by turning the handle on the reel. Within a couple of fishing trips, casting with a fixed spool reel will become second nature – more on casting later.

One feature of the fixed spool reel that is extremely useful is the drag. Drag is a safety mechanism that releases line from the spool just before the line breaks.

Drag is adjusted using the drag tensioner at the front or back or the reel.

The drag should be set to suit the strength of the line being used, ensuring that the drag will prevent the line from breaking.

A simple way to check the drag setting is to pull line from the reel and see if the drag releases before the line breaks (not scientific) or use a spring balance to tension the line and the drag to a known weight (very scientific).

Seek advice from the tackle dealer before buying a reel. Tell the dealer where you will be fishing and what methods you might use. If possible, try the reel on your rod. Above all, make sure the reel is the right size, and you can reach the spool with your fingertip.

Rig

Rig is the term used to describe the business end of the tackle: the hook, the weight/s, the hooklength, the knots, the connectors, and the feeder or float. We look at various rigs later in this book.

Line diameter	Breaking strain
0.06mm	12oz
0.07mm	1lb 2oz
0.08mm	1lb 12oz
0.09mm	2lb
0.10mm	2lb 6oz
0.11mm	2lb 14oz
0.12mm	3lb 4oz
0.14mm	4lb 12oz
0.16mm	5lb 10oz
0.18mm	6lb 8oz
0.20mm	7lb 12oz
0.22mm	9lb
0.24mm	10lb 4oz
0.26mm	11lb 6oz

Line

Fishing line is used to connect the angler, via the rod/pole, to the hookbait and (hopefully) the fish. The line must be strong enough to take the strain of the fish being caught, and thin enough not to be visible to the fish as they're feeding. And that's the dilemma – stronger lines are thicker and more visible; therefore, there has to be a compromise. The angler must use the thinnest line possible without increasing the risk of losing any fish. It's no use fishing for 40lb carp on 2lb line, for example.

The line to use is monofilament – it offers the best performance at the right price. Other line materials are available, such as fluorocarbon and braided lines, but these come at a cost.

To gain the maximum advantage from the different line qualities, most anglers would use mainline monofilament from the reel/pole and use a superior line for the hooklength. The hooklength is a short (6 to 24in) length of line tied to the hook and connected to the mainline.

Chart Two shows the typical lines to be used for each type of fish. For stillwater float fishing, I use a 2lb line for general fishing, with a slightly heavier line (maybe 4lb) if there were big tench and bream to be caught.

If I was targeting the larger bream and tench, I would go to 5lb line. For carp and pike, I use 15lb line. The chart below shows the typical monofilament line thicknesses and breaking strains.

Float

I started fishing over 45 years ago, and I still get excited when I see floats in a fishing tackle shop. There are so many colours, shapes and sizes; some, I swear, I've never seen before.

EQUIPMENT

The general rule with float fishing is to have a set of floats that can suit all the conditions you might encounter in the foreseeable future; don't buy floats for use on a fast-flowing river if you will fish the canal. Also, choose floats that you're able to see from a distance.

Despite the ever-increasing range of floats available, there are two basic designs for rod fishing – we'll cover pole floats separately.

For general fishing, there are two patterns of float with distinct ways of using them. The float is a simple stick, which is also called a host of other names – quill, peacock, avon, crystal, waggler, stick waggler, and so on.

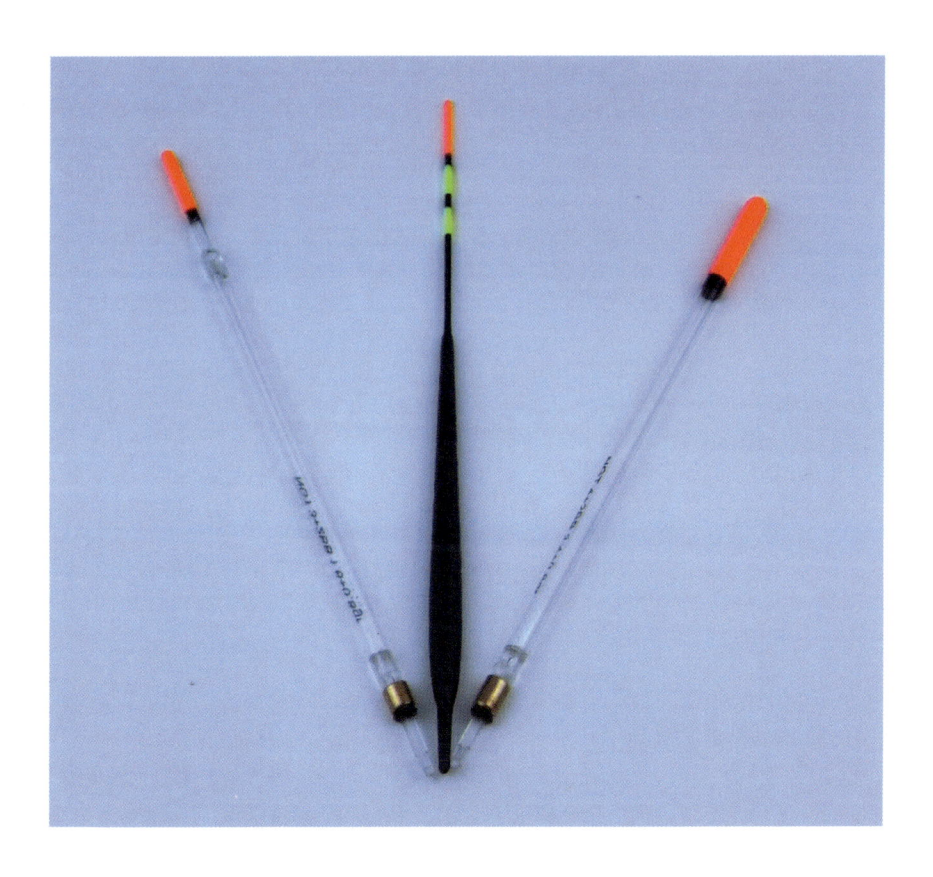

The floats displayed here, left to right, are:

A loaded insert crystal waggler

A bodied waggler

A loaded crystal waggler.

The two patterns of float are:

> Waggler, (see the previous page) which is straight or bodied (with a slightly bulbous section at the bottom of the float) to add stability in windy conditions. Wagglers come in all sizes and are generally used on stillwaters.
>
> Wagglers are attached to the line at the bottom of the float only, allowing the line between the float and the rod to be tightened for better float control and to combat the wind. Some wagglers are pre-loaded with weight, which makes them extremely aerodynamic and great for casting distances. Large pre-weighted (loaded) wagglers can be cast over 30 yards (although you might not be able to loosefeed that far).
>
> Stick float, which (again) is straight or bodied (with a slightly bulbous section at the top of the float) to add stability in fast-moving water. Stick floats come in all sizes and are generally used on rivers.
>
> Stick floats are attached to the line at the top and bottom of the float, allowing the line between the float and the rod to be controlled to combat the flow of water and for a better connection with the fish.

Pole floats are invariably much smaller and lighter than rod floats; because they don't get cast in the same way, there's simply no need for them to hold much weight. Some pole floats hold just 0.1g of weight, that's a single shot of 2mm diameter.

Most pole floats have a bulbous section towards the top of the float, the size of this section determines how much weight the float will carry. In calm conditions, on a stillwater, the selected float could be light, in gusty conditions a heavier float might be needed.

Like river fishing, the pole float is usually connected to the line at the top and bottom of the float.

I IMPORTANT:

Notice that any statistics or information relating to poles and pole tackle is in metric units, whereas rod tackle is in imperial units. It's slightly confusing, but that's the way it is, unfortunately.

There are IMPERIAL-METRIC conversion charts in Annex One.

One significant advantage of pole floats is that the entire rig (line, float, weight and hook) is prepared before the fishing session and connected to the pole elastic on the bank of the water. This considerably shortens the set-up time.

After the session, the rig is wound onto a winder and stored until the next session. The entire rig can also be swapped quickly and easily part way through the fishing session.

Weight

Let's talk about float fishing weights, or shot, before we cover legering weights – the two weights are entirely different.

Float Weights

Weight is essential for float fishing; it helps to present the hookbait to the fish and gives the angler more power in the cast.

The most popular weights for float fishing are shot (or split shot). As the name implies, the weight is shot (a small round ball of metal) with a split or cut in it. Some anglers may refer to lead shot because, until around 1986, the shot was sometimes manufactured from lead. Nowadays eco-friendly alternatives are used to protect the fish and other aquatic life.

Split shot comes in all sizes from the large 3SSG (4.8g) to a tiny Number 13 (0.01g). The shot is designated with letters and numbers, the higher the number, the smaller the shot and the lower the weight – see Annex One.

The shot is attached to the line between the float and the hook, by nipping the line in the split. The shot is sometimes used either side of the float to keep it in place.

The position of the shot between the float and the hook, causes the bait to behave differently. More on shotting later in the book.

Shotting the float until it becomes a tiny dot will produce more bites as the fish feel less resistance.

When the correct weight has been added to the line, the float will sit correctly in the water with only the tip of the float remaining visible. With the float in the correct position, the fish feels minimum resistance as it takes the hookbait. So, weight plays a vital part in the hookbait presentation and bite detection.

Leger weights

Legering is an alternative method to float fishing, typically used to catch larger fish from the bottom of the water and is almost exclusively used for specimen fish such as carp, barbel and wels catfish.

Legering consists of a weight to hold the hookbait to the bottom, and a method of bite detection such as a soft rod tip or another bite detector.

A leger weight can take many forms, from a simple 'ball' to a bunch of large shot. Feeders could also be considered a form of leger weight.

Feeder

Feeders are synonymous with specimen fish especially carp, bream, tench and barbel.

A feeder is simply a weight, used for legering, that carries groundbait or loosefeed.

Feeder fishing generally requires the use of heavier tackle (rod and line) to cope with the additional weight of the feeder and its contents. Nothing is gained from casting a feeder 40 yards for it to snap the line through its sheer weight and momentum.

Feeders simply distribute loosefeed and groundbait around the hookbait; although some are also used to transport the hookbait itself.

There is a variety of feeder types, with more being developed constantly, these include:

Cage feeder – a wire mesh tube stuffed with loosefeed and groundbait; the feed falls out of the tube as the feeder falls through the water.

   A cage feeder is a great way to get loosefeed and groundbait into the swim.

Blockend feeder – a plastic tube stuffed with loosefeed (maggots) and blocked with groundbait; the feed makes its way out of the feeder as the groundbait dissipates.

   Ideal for rivers, as the flow slowly disperses the groundbait.

Maggot feeder – a perforated plastic tube filled with maggots; the loosefeed exits the feeder and leaves a carpet of feed around the hookbait.

Method feeder – the ultimate 'carp catcher', is a tray loaded with loosefeed, groundbait and the hookbait; by using a mould, the loosefeed can be moulded onto feeder along with the hookbait.

   As the fish feed from the feeder, they will (hopefully) take the hookbait.

PVA bag – since the bag dissolves, it's not strictly a feeder, but still an effective method of loosefeed delivery.

GOING FISHING

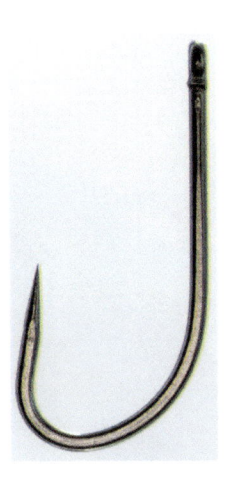

Hook

Let's talk about hooks; anyone new to fishing might wonder what there is to talk about – a hook is a hook; right?

Hooks come in a multitude of sizes; the most popular hooks vary from a number 26, which is tiny (about 1.5mm across the gap), to a number 2, which is large - about 10mm across the gap (or bigger for sea fishing).

Hooks are sold in even number sizes only, but I'm assured that the odd number sizes are also available – I've never seen them. In my tackle box, for general use, I carry hook sizes from no. 24 through to no. 10.

I always use barbless hooks, although some anglers like to use barbed hooks, micro-barbed and whisker-barbed hooks. The barb is a small protrusion behind the point, which prevents the hook from coming loose. Barbless hooks tend to cause less harm to the fish than barbed hooks.

Hooks also come in a range of variants to suit the hookbait being used: coloured hooks, different shank lengths, and wide gap (or gape). Hooks can also be eyed or spade end. They have an eye (or hole) at the top for threading the line through and tying, or they have a flattened end requiring the use of a specific knot (such as the Domhoff knot) to connect the line to the hook. Spade end hooks usually need a small hook-tying tool to assist in the knot-making.

PAGE 38

Other Gear

Disgorger

The purpose of a disgorger is to remove fishing hooks quickly and safely from the fish.

Typically, a disgorger comprises a loop device at the end of a short metal or plastic rod, some designs have a notch to push the barb out.

To use a disgorger, thread the loop onto the line (keeping the line tight) and push towards the hook until it comes free. Gently remove the hook and the disgorger from the fish's mouth. It sounds easy, but it takes practice as the hook can sometimes be inaccessible.

I carry a range of disgorger designs to be sure that I can always get to the hook however inaccessible it may seem to be.

For larger fish, especially those with teeth, it's worth investing in a pair of surgical forceps. The forceps allow greater access where necessary, reducing the risk of harm to the fish. Barbless hooks are generally easier to remove than barbed hooks.

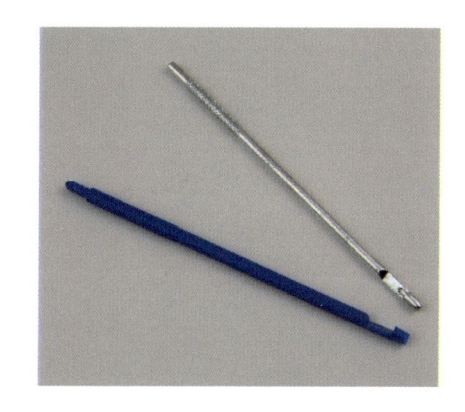

Plummet

A plummet is a small weight clipped onto the end of the line, when float fishing, to set the correct distance between the float tip and the hook.

The distance often matches the depth of the water.

By plumbing the water in many places around your 'swim', you will develop an impression of the shape of the bottom – any ledges, troughs, and so on.

Float stop

Float stops are an alternative to split shot to secure the position of a float; they're moulded rubber balls, with a hole through, which are used either side of the float to keep it in place.

Chinagraph pencil

You might ask why you should need a chinagraph pencil. The answer is, to simply mark your fishing depth after plumbing the water and setting your float stops.

By hooking your hook around the reel seat or first ring and tightening the line, you can mark the rod to show where the top of the float is. In the event of retackling your rod, there's no need to plumb the depth again.

A chinagraph pencil is made from a hard wax, like a wax crayon. The marks are removed with a paper towel and leave no scratches or stains.

Catapult

Catapults are often necessary to get loosefeed and groundbait to the right place in your swim.

As expected, there is a vast range of catapults available, each with different characteristics – size, weight, elasticity, and so on.

For a beginner, decide what you want to use the catapult for (loosefeed or groundbait) and purchase one you can afford and get used to it by practising to get the loosefeed or groundbait close to where you're fishing.

It takes time but continued frequent use of your catapult will pay off.

Tackle box

All the tackle we've mentioned so far: reels, line (on spare spools), floats, split shot, leger weights, feeders, hooks, disgorgers, plummets, float stops, and catapults, needs to be carried to the waterside. The most effective way of carrying your tackle, without the risk of it being damaged, is in a tackle box.

Tackle boxes range from simple plastic trays with multiple compartments and a lid, to cantilevered plastic 'toolboxes', and to seat boxes with trays and drawers.

Choose a tackle box that suits your needs but with room for expansion – the tackle you carry will increase; so, take account of that when buying a tackle box. Also, consider that it must be carried to the waterside, which means you need to choose something practical.

A ADVICE:

I use an inexpensive seat box, with smaller tackle boxes inside. It allows me to carry all the tackle I need and, since it has a shoulder strap, I have my hands free to carry bait, nets, rods, banksticks, poles, and so on.

Landing net

A landing net is necessary to lift the fish out of the water. It is an essential piece of equipment; without it, the fish suffer. The landing net looks like a larger version of a kid's fishing net – a small net on a hoop at the end of a pole. Landing nets come in three shapes – rectangle, circle or triangle. I can't say any has an advantage over the others. Try to get a net at least 15in across, with a handle over 6ft long.

I IMPORTANT:

Some fisheries specify the minimum size of the landing net; check before you fish.

Keepnet

Some fisheries and waters don't allow keepnets unless match fishing; check your permit first.

If used incorrectly, a keepnet can damage the fish; so, care is required when selecting, locating and using your keepnet.

GOING FISHING

A keepnet is used to retain the caught fish so they can be released at the end of the fishing session. In a match, the fish are weighed before being released.

There is much debate about the need for a keepnet: OK, they could cause harm to the fish, they could spread disease between waters, and they smell!

It is extremely satisfying to empty a keepnet at the end of a session (if there are many fish in it).

If you want to use a keepnet, aim to invest in a micromesh rectangular net around 10ft long.

For carp anglers, using keepnets is slightly more complicated. Many fishing clubs, fisheries and waters specify a limit on the number of carp in a keepnet – often with a 50lb limit per net. PLUS, most also determine that silver fish (freshwater fish other than carp) must be kept in a separate keepnet.

This policy doesn't reduce the use of keepnets; it often requires three or more keepnets per fishing session.

Bankstick

Banksticks are metal tubes of rods with a point at one end, and a (female) threaded portion at the other.

Some are fixed length of around 18 to 24 in, although extendable banksticks are much more popular (and more expensive).

Banksticks are typically used to hold rod rests and any other equipment to be raised off the ground and made accessible to the angler, such as bait boxes and tackle trays.

A ADVICE:

I normally carry eight banksticks; four of those are extendable.

Rod rest

Rod rests are invariably made from plastic and are used with banksticks or similar arrangements to support fishing rods.

Generally, two rod rests are required for each rod, although I use my seat box as the rear rod rest, and a large scooped rest for the front part of my rod.

Some rod rests are simply a metal rod with a plastic V on top; these should be avoided since they aren't sturdy, bend easily, and are not so easy to see – which is probably why I find so many that have been left behind by anglers.

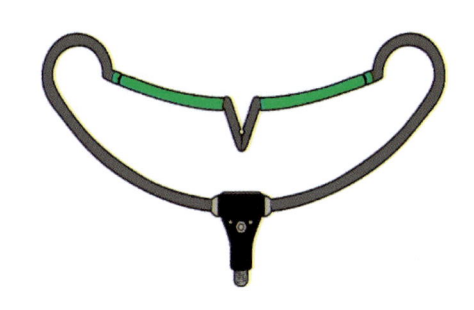

Pole roller

A pole roller is a free-standing device that allows a pole to be rolled over it without causing damage to the pole.

The pole roller is essential equipment when the pole must be pulled back from the water; with the weight at the butt end, the pole quickly becomes unbalanced.

Using a pole roller to support the pole makes the pole movement smoother, less tiresome, and prevents damage to the pole.

Bite alarm

Bite alarms are mainly used for specimen fish, especially carp.

The device sits in a bankstick, acting as a rod rest, and detecting any movement of the line. Bites are indicated by an audible (and sometimes visual) alarm.

Bait box

Bait boxes are essential for keeping live baits (maggots, casters, worms, pinkies, feeders, gozzers, jokers, and so on) fresh, and for transporting the bait to the waterside.

Bait boxes are typically made from plastic, with a tight-fitting perforated lid.

Holdalls

We already mentioned the tackle and equipment required to catch fish; it might sound daunting, but it isn't.

However, you must always remember that the tackle and equipment must be transported to the water's edge. Plan; how are you going to do that?

Holdalls of all types are often used to get nets, baits, rods, poles, etc. to the water.

Trolley

When people go overseas on holiday, they would generally take around 33lb to 40lb of belongings. A typical match angler arriving at their swim, for a five-hour match, would have around four or five times that weight.

Don't try to carry all your tackle from your car to the swim, if necessary make two trips or use a trolley. A small foldable trolley could be handy. Select a trolley that fits in your car alongside all the rest of your equipment – a foldable trolley is best if space is tight. Select and pack your tackle wisely before each trip – only carry the tackle you need (plus baits, etc.).

ADVICE:

Assess all the options; don't go for the branded holdalls initially. A rod holdall might cost you anything from a few pounds to a couple of hundred pounds; consider which might be most suitable.

Bowl

Bowls are essential for mixing groundbait or loosefeed at the water's edge. Always purchase bowls that are flexible, easy to clean and inexpensive. Choose bowls with a capacity of between 4 and 6 litres.

Unhooking mat

When handling larger fish, it's wise to use an unhooking mat, which is simply a padded sheet that's kept wet to avoid damaging the fish.

Beginners wouldn't usually be concerned about such equipment unless larger fish were being targeted.

IMPORTANT:

Some fisheries insist on using unhooking mats – check before you fish - don't get caught without one!

Bait

Bait is a term to describe something that should attract fish. In this section, we cover hookbaits (the bait on the hook), in the following sections we will talk about groundbait (powdered feed deposited in the fishing area) and loosefeed (particles of bait deposited in the fishing area).

In Chart Three, we identified a range of common hookbaits: maggot, caster, worms, bread, corn and boilies. Here we expand the range and add detail to help you get the best out of the bait.

We can categorise baits into larvae, pupae, worms, bread, particles, pellets, meat, pet food, molluscs, berries and boilies. Most anglers have their favourite baits, just like most fish have their favourite foods. The best baits vary from water to water and also depend on the weather.

That's why many anglers carry a selection of baits, anticipating the fish will like some of them. So, a little research on the place you've chosen to fish will pay dividends – what bait are anglers using?

Larvae

Larvae hatch from the eggs of flies, they come in many forms (pinkies, squats, gozzers, etc.) but the most common is the maggot. Maggots are the most widely used fishing bait in the UK – literally thousands of gallons each day. The other larvae are less popular and often more expensive.

Maggots are usually available in a range of colours; it's impossible to say which is best, so I usually get a box of white and a box of multi-coloured.

Always keep your maggots in a box designed for larvae (these are available at all tackle shops). This allows the bait to breathe and not to sweat.

The best way to present a maggot is to hook it at the flat end by nicking the edge of the skin – avoid bursting the maggot. Always use a sharp, fine wire hook (size 18 or 20). Otherwise, the maggot will be difficult to hook properly. Maggots are used singly, in pairs, and in bunches.

Pinkies are smaller than maggots and tend to be used as hookbait for smaller fish, or for loosefeeding.

Squats are smaller than maggots and pinkies, as such they're hardly used as hookbaits except on those days when all else has failed – the winter match when nothing is biting.

Larvae need care to keep them in good condition. It's a good idea to riddle your bait and keep the flour clean – some anglers do this a couple of times before using the bait and then every two to three days.

Maggots must be kept clean, dry and at a low temperature.

Another type of larvae bait is gozzers, this a term often used to describe maggots that have been bred at home. It's a little messy when you're harvesting the larvae, and extremely smelly - so it's best done at about three miles from your home.

IMPORTANT:

I just want to mention the importance of keeping the larvae dry. Wet maggots suddenly gain amazing powers to crawl vertically on any surface; pinkies are worse.

Pupae

Pupae are the chrysalises of larvae – known as casters. So, keep your maggots in good condition for a week or so, and they'll stop moving before turning into an orange, and then red/brown, cocoon.

However, casters are normally purchased in a sealed plastic bag and are generally better than those that have 'turned' at home.

Keep casters in a bait box, with an airtight cover. However, at the waterside half-fill the box with water to keep the casters submerged and cool. Refresh the water every couple of hours. The water also identifies the casters that are floating (usually the darker ones) – these make a terrible loosefeed but can be used as a floating hookbait.

Casters must be hooked by the flat end, but not the same as a maggot; the hook (size 10 or 20) needs to be pushed into the shell of the caster. Again, a sharp fine hook is needed – avoid bursting the caster, discard any that are oozing liquid.

Worms

Worms of all sizes have been used as fishing bait for hundreds of years.

Generally, worms are thought to be easy to find and free – simply collect them (usually lobworms) from any close-mown grass on a wet night (a torch is needed).

You can also dig for worms in a garden (get permission first), in a compost heap or a manure heap (usually brandlings).

If you need lots of worms, consider setting-up a wormery (usually with redworms) – a simple wormery can be built in your garden or purchased for around £70, and they don't need constant care and maintenance.

> Try cutting off the end of the worm to allow the worm juice to flow into the water.

Worms are used whole, depending on their size, or cut into usable pieces for hookbait. Chopped worms are used as loosefeed. Typically, hook sizes from 18 (for brandlings) to 12 (for lobworms) should be used. I normally hook the bait about one-third along its length.

Worms should be kept in damp moss or damp grass cuttings – never let the worms go dry. Store the container in a cool, dry place away from heat and direct sunlight.

A quick word on bloodworms; bloodworms are not worms, but they have a worm-like appearance - they are the larvae of midges. Bloodworms are found in the silt of stillwaters and are extracted by using a blunt blade to scrape them from the silt. They can be ordered from your local tackle shop or purchased online.

When using light tackle (size 24 hook), the bloodworm is an unbeatable bait for small bream and roach. That's why bloodworms are banned on many waters – check your permit before you fish.

Bread

Bread is an extremely versatile fishing bait, which is used as hookbait and groundbait. As a hookbait, bread needs no preparation, simply pull the type of bread bait you require from the loaf or slice.

> Floating bread is often banned; it prevents the ducks being caught as they sample the free offerings.

Bread flake is pulled from the centre of a fresh loaf, the hook (size 16 or 14) is pushed through the flake, and the flake is pinched onto the shank of the hook. Bread flake is great for roach and rudd.

Bread crust is hooked in the same way but is used to catch fish on the surface.

EQUIPMENT

Punched bread is a popular hookbait for match anglers; using a small tool (called a bread punch), small circular pellets of bread can be cut from a slice and placed directly on the hook.

Try fishing with punched bread as hookbait with breadcrumbs as groundbait; it's often unbeatable.

I find that punched bread sometimes falls off the hook during the cast. My solution is to 'prepare' the bread in advance:

- In your kitchen, remove the crusts from a slice of bread,
- Place the slice in a microwave for five seconds,
- Remove swiftly and immediately flatten with a rolling pin,
- Place in a sealed bag until you get to the water's edge.

When you use your bread punch, you will find the flattened bread easier to hook; it will swell to its regular size in the water.

If you don't have a bread punch, follow the steps above, but cut the bread into small squares before placing in the sealed bag.

Bread paste makes an effective hookbait; the paste takes only seconds to prepare:

- Remove the crust from the bread,
- Place the bread in a piece of fabric,
- Wet the fabric parcel,
- Squeeze the water from the parcel,
- Open the parcel to reveal the bread paste.

By keeping the bread covered, the paste remains fresh.

Bread paste can be pinched onto the hook leaving the point exposed.

> **IMPORTANT:**
>
> All particle baits must be prepared by soaking or cooking before being used.

Particles

Particle baits encompass a vast array of nuts, beans, peas, cereals, seeds, pulses, legumes, and derivatives.

Some particles baits are sold in metal containers; transfer the contents to an air-tight container before your fishing trip. Do not take metal containers to the water.

The most popular particle, which needs no preparation, is processed sweetcorn. Transfer the contents of the can to a sealable bait box, and that's it.

Hemp, which is a good hookbait and loosefeed, can be bought ready prepared, as can a lot of the particles – I think it's better to buy prepared particles rather than trying to do the cooking at home.

Pellets

Pellets are extremely popular (and successful) bait on some waters; pellets are available in an extensive range of sizes, colours, flavours, and textures.

Hard pellets can be used as loosefeed or groundbait (mixed with water), soft pellets can be used as hookbait.

Many fisheries stock their own highly nutritious pellets and ban the use of all others – check before you fish.

Pellets are used across many species of fish from roach to carp, and on all types of water from canals to fast rivers.

The vast range of pellets allows anglers to experiment and, at less than £3 for a resealable tub, they make a great ready-to-use bait.

Meat

Meat was a very popular bait, but introducing boilies persuaded anglers to leave the meat behind. Luncheon meat is still used for larger fish, such as carp or barbel, and is easy to use. Simply take the meat from the tin, cut it into useable hookbaits or loosefeed and transfer the meat into a sealable bait box. Keep it refrigerated until you're ready to go fishing. Other meats are worthy of consideration for larger fish; sausages, for example, especially the one I mentioned earlier (Pepperami).

ADVICE:

Most processed meats are sold in metal cans; transfer the contents to an air-tight container before your fishing trip. Do not take metal containers to the water.

Pet food

Pet food is often worth a try, especially for carp. Try Coshida cat food (other brands are available), it's firm and stays on the hook – other brands must be mixed with meal to make them stick to the hook. To attract surface-feeding carp, try dry cat food or dog food - with a few loose tempters the sport is extremely fast and exciting. The bait, due to its hardness, often needs to be banded or hair-rigged to the hook.

Molluscs

Molluscs, such as slugs, can be used in fast-flowing rivers, especially after a spell of rain. They are a great bait for chub, and occasionally for barbel.

Berries

Berries, especially those growing naturally on the banks of the water, can be used as hookbait. Grab a few to tempt the fish when all other baits fail.

Boilies

Boilies are the dominant fishing bait, especially for specimen anglers. They are used as hookbait and as loosefeed. In my view, boilies have changed fishing forever.

Boilies are manufactured from meals, flours, proteins, seeds, flavours and a binding agent (usually egg). Boilies are available in a vast range of sizes, colours and flavours. Many anglers have their favourite boilies, so it's worth experimenting.

When you're fishing, look at what boilies other anglers are using, and see what fish they're catching. The larger boilies often catch the larger fish.

Since boilies are a hard bait, they must be fished on a hair rig, which allows the bait to be presented alongside the hook. Simply, the boilie is threaded onto the hair (an extension to the hooklength) which provides a more natural presentation.

Artificial Hookbaits

Artificial hookbaits are moulded plastic replicas of the natural hookbaits. The main advantage is their durability; storage is not an issue – they stay fresh forever.

Sweetcorn, maggots, worms and hemp are the most popular artificial baits – but artificial pellets and bread are also available.

While some successful anglers promote the widespread use of artificial baits, I remain sceptical. I prefer the natural approach.

I will not dismiss the use of artificial baits; I'm sure sometimes they're useful.

Some fisheries ban artificial baits – check before you fish.

Deadbait

Deadbait is the term used to describe whole, or parts of, dead fish used to catch predator fish. The fish can be freshwater fish or sea fish.

Livebait

Livebait is small live fish, typically from the venue being fished, used to catch predator fish.

Groundbait

Groundbait is generally a wet powdered bait deposited in the fishing area, as opposed to loosefeed which is often particles of bait (or bait samples) deposited in the fishing area. Anglers sometimes combine the two to provide an attractant with samples of the hookbait.

Groundbait is used to attract fish into your swim. The groundbait mix can be light to form a cloud, or heavy to form a carpet of feed (or both).

Typically, groundbait contains a range of ground-up attractants such as breadcrumbs, fishmeal, pellets, potatoes, hemp, birdseed, colouring, flavouring, and so on.

Many anglers have their favourite mix; others are content to buy the ready-blended groundbait from their tackle shop.

Groundbait is dry when purchased or made; it's transported to the waterside dry in bags, buckets or mixing bowls.

At the waterside, small batches of groundbait are prepared by hand using the water at the venue and around 1lb of dry mix.

IMPORTANT:

Some fisheries don't allow the use of livebait so check before you fish.

Try making groundbait with the water from a can of sweetcorn; the added flavour can make a lot of difference.

Use a shallow mixing container to allow even distribution of water and add the water little by little until the required consistency of groundbait is achieved, i.e. it holds tightly together when squeezed but also falls apart easily without forming lumps.

Groundbait is pressed into balls (from golf ball size to tennis ball size) to provide a projectile which is tossed into the water. Generally, the harder the ball is pressed, the firmer it becomes.

Groundbait can also be used with a feeder, which provides accurate delivery of the bait into the swim.

Ground-baiting by hand takes practice, the mix must be right, so the balls hold together, and the throw must be accurate – more on this later.

Loosefeed

Loosefeed is often particles of bait (or bait samples) deposited in the fishing area.

Loosefeed is used to attract fish into your swim, and to encourage them to feed. But you don't want the fish to eat until they're no longer hungry. Otherwise they won't be interested in your hookbait.

When loosefeeding, I avoid using the hookbait as a loosefeed – in my view, the loosefeed makes my bait indistinguishable.

I want my hookbait to stand out, so I would normally use smaller bait samples for loosefeeding:

> If I'm fishing with maggots, I will feed pinkies;
>
> If I'm fishing with worms, I will feed chopped worms;
>
> If I'm fishing with bread, I will feed breadcrumbs, and so on.

EQUIPMENT

Knots

Knots are important and often neglected; knots weaken the line. So, the correct knot, tied properly, and used for a specific purpose, reduces the risk of line breakage.

Some anglers have a large portfolio of knots they can call upon to tie things together. Other anglers, me included, rely upon three or four knots to cover a range of applications.

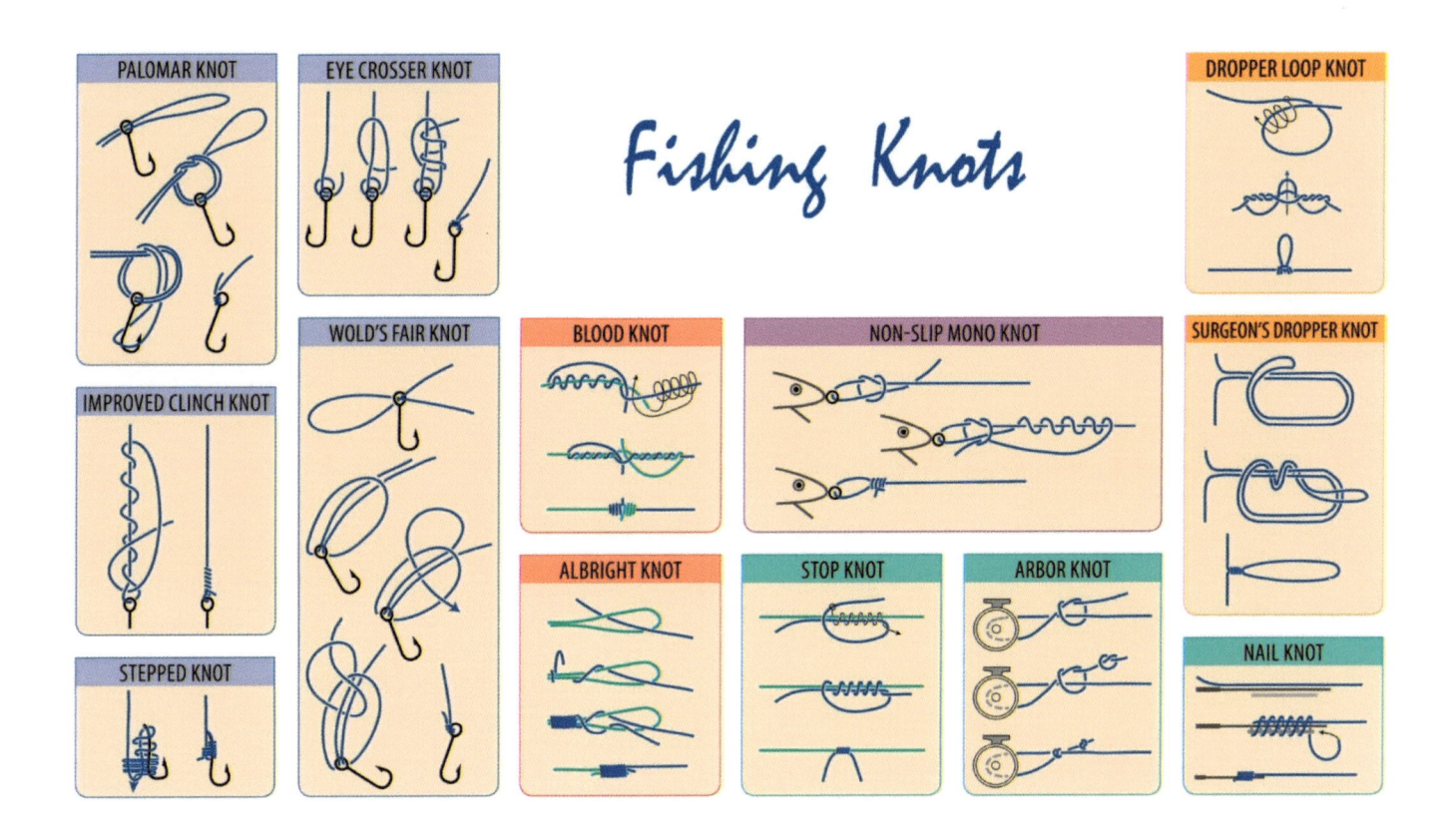

Fishing Knots

The following pages contain details of the knots I normally use and their specific purpose.

PAGE 55

FIGURE OF EIGHT

The figure of eight is a classic knot that can be relied upon in many circumstances.

The knot is used for creating loops (obviously) to make quick link attachments.

ALWAYS WET YOUR KNOT BEFORE PULLING TIGHT

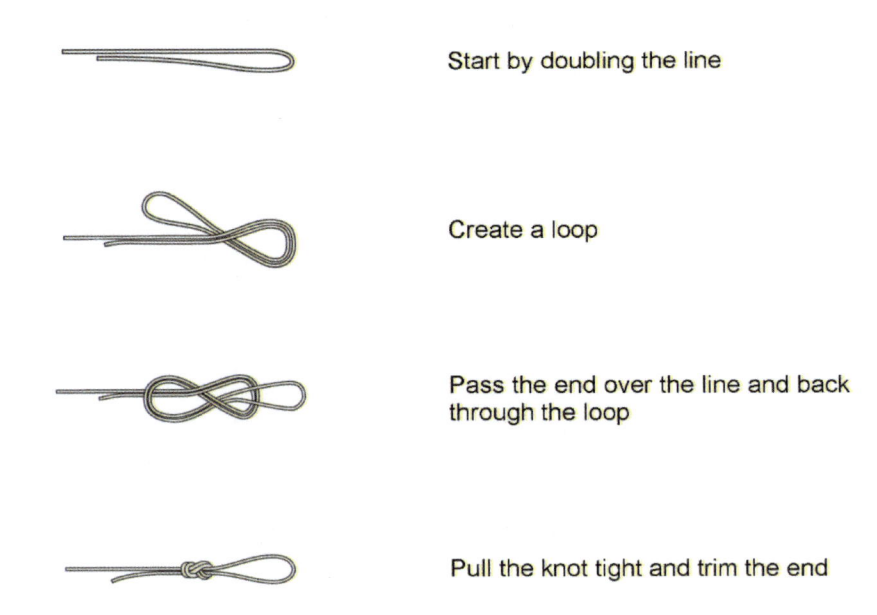

Start by doubling the line

Create a loop

Pass the end over the line and back through the loop

Pull the knot tight and trim the end

EQUIPMENT

GRINNER

The grinner is a reliable strong knot that can be used in all circumstances where hooks and other tackle need to be attached.

ALWAYS WET YOUR KNOT BEFORE PULLING TIGHT

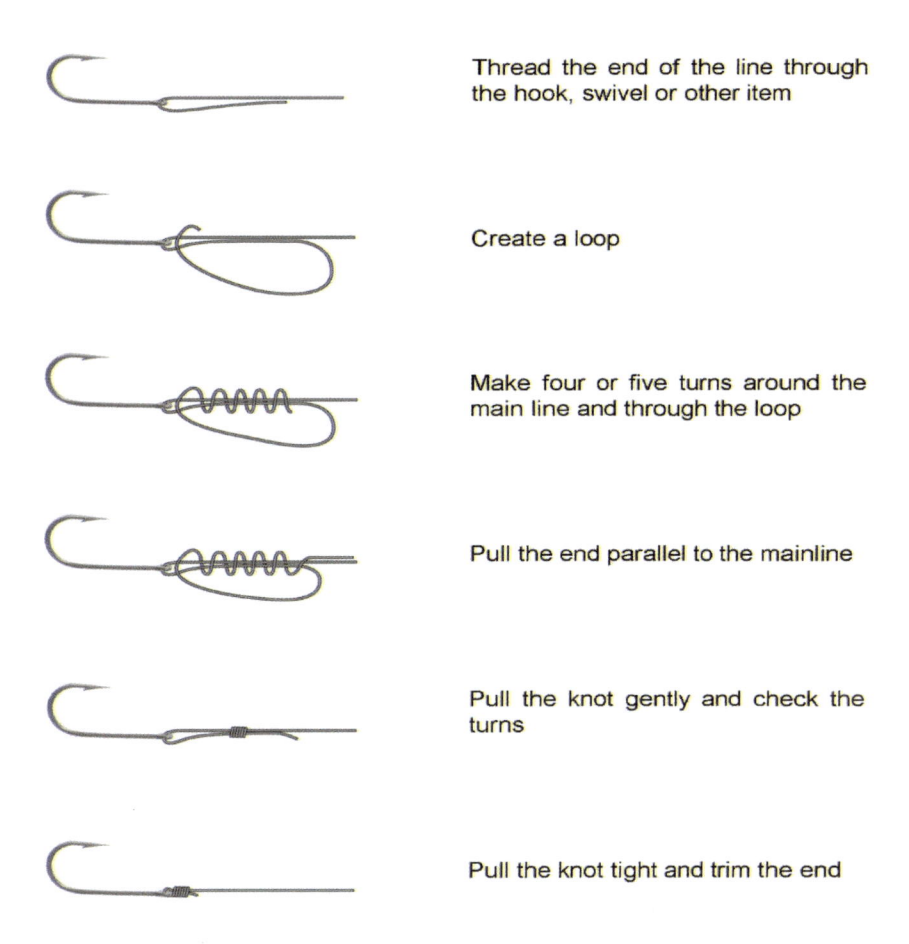

Thread the end of the line through the hook, swivel or other item

Create a loop

Make four or five turns around the main line and through the loop

Pull the end parallel to the mainline

Pull the knot gently and check the turns

Pull the knot tight and trim the end

HALF BLOOD

The half blood is a reliable and well-known knot that can be used for attaching hooks and other terminal tackle, as well as creating line-to-line attachments.

ALWAYS WET YOUR KNOT BEFORE PULLING TIGHT

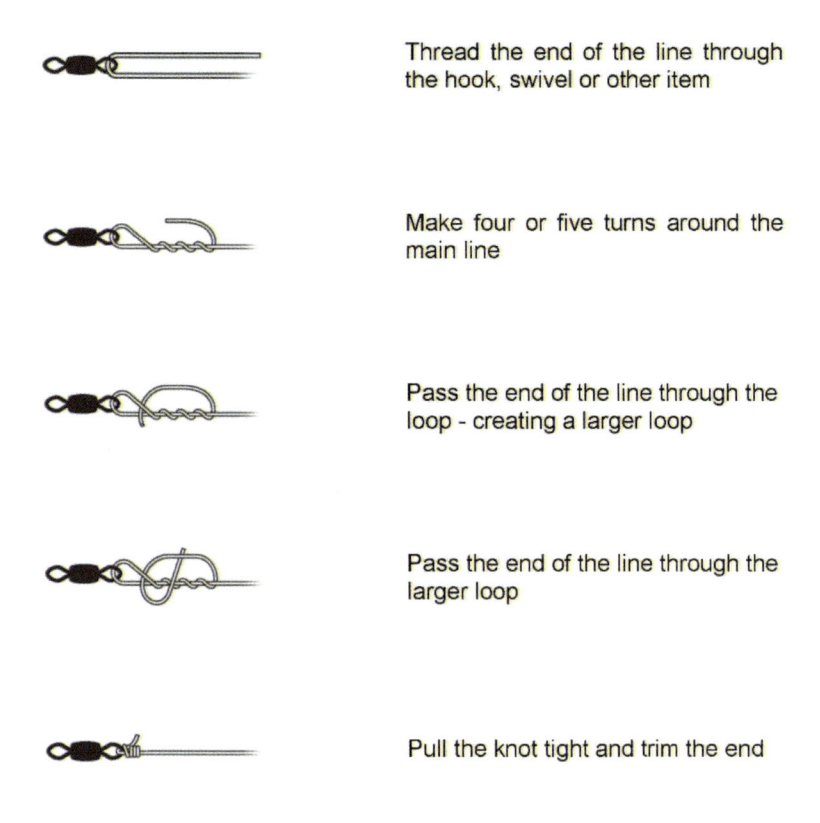

Thread the end of the line through the hook, swivel or other item

Make four or five turns around the main line

Pass the end of the line through the loop - creating a larger loop

Pass the end of the line through the larger loop

Pull the knot tight and trim the end

PALOMAR

The palomar is possibly the most useful knot - it is easy to tie and can be used for all types of terminal tackle.

If pulled tight correctly, the knot loses less than 10% of the line strength. Check that the knot is tightened evenly.

ALWAYS WET YOUR KNOT BEFORE PULLING TIGHT

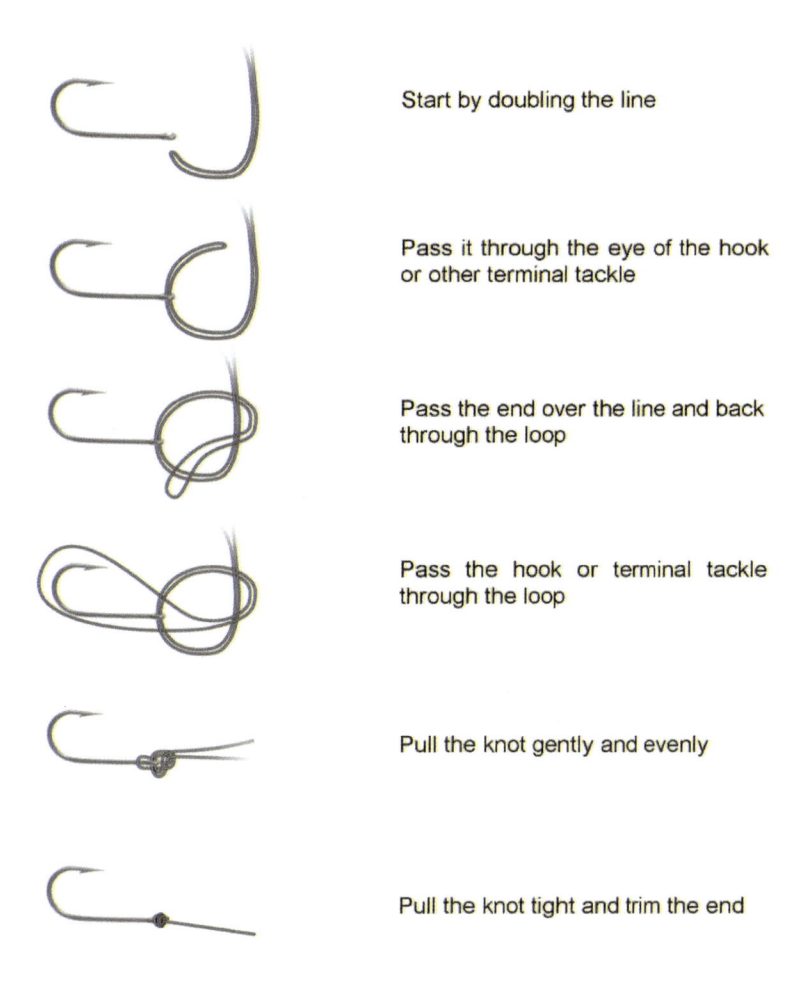

Start by doubling the line

Pass it through the eye of the hook or other terminal tackle

Pass the end over the line and back through the loop

Pass the hook or terminal tackle through the loop

Pull the knot gently and evenly

Pull the knot tight and trim the end

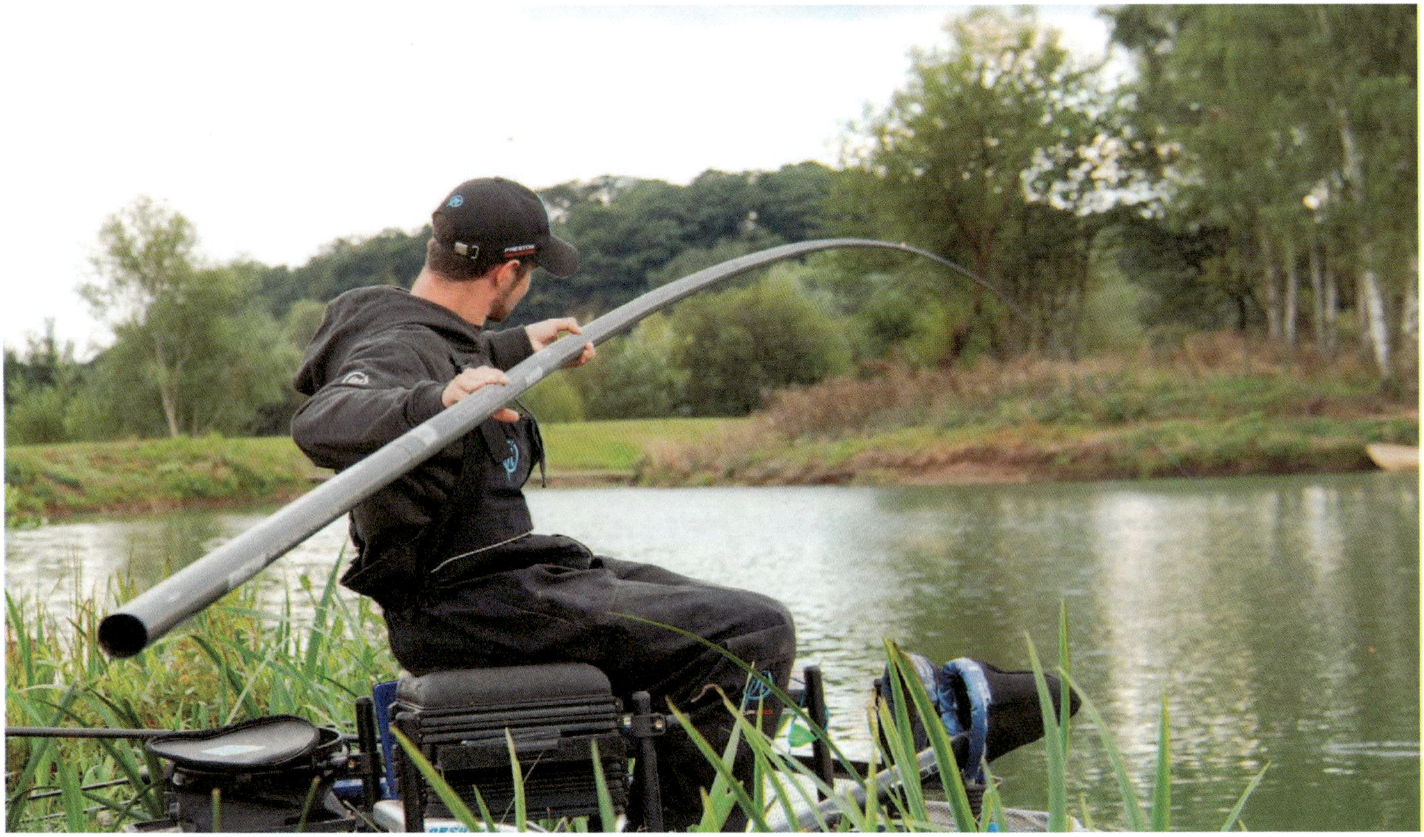

FOUR: Where to fish and the methods to use

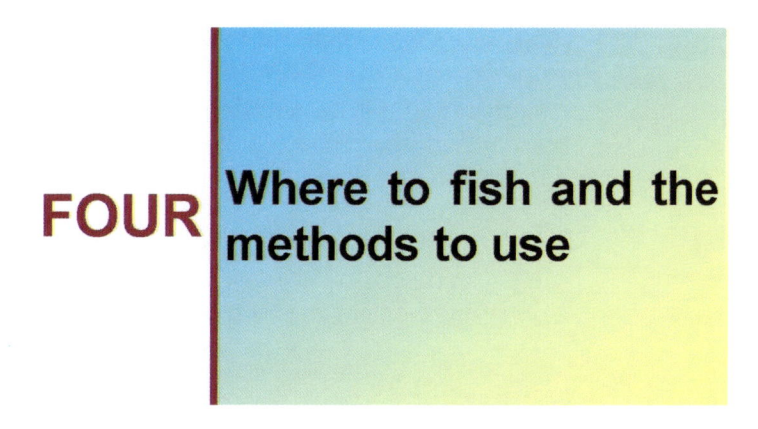

In this section, we cover the different types of water to be fished and the different methods that might be adopted for each. We expand on the information outlined in Charts One, Two and Three. We can't cover all types of water, in all conditions, for each method and each fish. So, here I'll summarise where the fish might be and how we might catch them.

Canals

Canals are man-made waterways designed and used to transport materials and products between major cities and key ports.

Nowadays the canals are mainly used by pleasure craft, and the towpaths are used by walkers, runners, cyclists and anglers.

In the UK, canals vary in width between 30ft and 50ft and have a depth between 3ft and 6ft.

Parts of the canal network are wider than 50ft – these often provide great fishing spots since the water is often not disturbed by passing boats.

A ADVICE:

When selecting a place to fish, choose somewhere that's not too close to tunnels and locks. Watch the movement of water before you choose where to fish. Either side of a bridge can produce fish.

GOING FISHING

Most of the 2,200 miles of navigable canal network provide excellent fishing opportunities. Canals are convenient for many people, are relatively easy to fish, and are usually very affordable.

Let's look at how we might fish a canal. Mostly, canals are stillwaters, but depending on the distance from tunnels, bridges and locks; anglers can experience flow as the boats move around.

All canals have a channel running down the middle; it's created by the movement of boats and provides the deepest part of the canal. There are usually two margins, one on each side of the canal where the water is shallow; the margins drop into the boat channel creating shelves (or slopes).

The shelf is often where the fish feed, especially when the wash of the passing boats pushes food to the edges of the centre channel. So, don't fish in the middle of the channel, opt to fish on the near or far slope.

As you're choosing your swim, look for fish moving on the surface, look for overhanging trees, look for reed beds, and watch for any feature (including moored boats) that might be used as shelter by fish.

ADVICE:

Always keep the canal towpath tidy, move rods and poles away from the passing traffic: runners, walkers and cyclists.

The best way to fish a canal is using a float, either on a rod or on a pole. Use a rod or whip for the near shelf, and a rod or pole for the far shelf. Keep the tackle light.

After you've selected your swim, plumb the depth – find the edges of the channel and the bottom of the shelves. Mark the depth on your rod/pole using a chinagraph pencil.

It's not necessary to fill the swim with groundbait and loosefeed – you will overfeed the fish, and they won't be interested in your bait. Keep the feed light, and let the fish come to your swim. If you're failing to catch, go for lighter tackle – a size 20 or 22 hook, maybe.

Bait: Use maggots, casters, worms, bread and corn. Use deadbaits and lures for the predators.

Expect to catch: roach, perch, rudd, bream, silver bream, tench, carp, and occasionally pike, zander and eels.

I IMPORTANT:

Fish from the canal towpath only don't be tempted to fish from the opposite bank.

Lakes

Try groundbaiting heavily (3 to 5 balls) at the beginning of your session. If possible, pre-bait the swim the day before you fish.

Lakes are formed naturally, they vary in size from small ponds to large inland seas.

In this section, we will mainly concentrate on man-made 'lakes' (reservoirs, gravel pits and quarries) that can be fished from the bank and are often no more than 20ft deep. There are thousands of such stillwaters dotted through the UK, each with its unique qualities. In fact, most stillwater fisheries are man-made lakes.

Let's look at how we might fish a lake. Lakes are stillwaters, although some lakes are fed by a water inlet, which could create a localised flow especially after heavy rain.

When selecting your swim, look for fish moving on the surface, look for overhanging trees, look for the reed beds, and watch for any feature that might be used as shelter by fish. Islands are a favourite, especially the slope into the water.

Lakes are fished using a float either on a rod or a pole, or by using a feeder. The choice depends on the fish being targeted, the depth of the water and the size of the lake.

If you're using a float, after you've selected your swim, you must plumb the depth – discover the underwater terrain and determine how deep you will fish. Mark the depth on your rod using a chinagraph pencil.

On some lakes, introducing lots of groundbait and loosefeed is necessary to get the fish into the swim. Introduce further groundbait and/or loosefeed little and often – let the fishing develop. If you're failing to catch, go for lighter tackle – a smaller hook, maybe.

Bait: Use maggots, casters, worms, bread and corn. Use deadbaits and lures for the predators.

Expect to catch: roach, perch, rudd, bream, silver bream, tench, carp, and occasionally pike, zander and eels.

Slow-moving rivers

Slow-moving rivers are natural waterways across flat land. Some are used by pleasure craft, and the paths alongside are used by walkers, runners, cyclists and anglers.

In the UK, slow-moving rivers vary in width between a 5ft and 300ft and have a depth between 3ft and 40ft. Parts of the river network are wider than 500ft – these are mainly tidal and inaccessible.

Let's look at how we might fish a slow-moving river. In many respects it's like fishing a canal, but with an ever-present flow.

When selecting your swim, look for fish moving on the surface, look for overhanging trees, look for the reed beds, and watch for any feature that might be used as shelter by fish.

> Rivers constantly change: the flow, colour and temperature are dictated by what's happening upstream. Always be prepared to change your tactics to suit the conditions.

The best way to fish a slow-moving river depends on the speed of the flow and of its width. For small rivers use a float, either with a rod or a pole. Use a rod, pole or whip for the near bank, and maybe a rod or pole for the far bank.

For wider and deeper rivers, a feeder might be the best solution to get out into the middle of the river. Again, depending on the speed of the flow, the river might contain carp or barbel – choose your method, tactics and bait accordingly.

After you've selected your swim, plumb the depth – find the contours, the channels, and the sandbanks. Mark the depth on your rod using a chinagraph pencil.

ADVICE:

Always keep the riverbank tidy, keep rods and poles away from the passing traffic: runners, walkers and cyclists.

Don't overfeed the fish with groundbait or loosefeed - let the fish find the free offerings. If you're failing to catch, go for lighter tackle.

Bait: Use maggots, worms, corn, bread, and pellets. Use deadbaits and lures for the predators.

Expect to catch: roach, perch, rudd, bream, silver bream, tench, carp, and occasionally pike, zander and eels.

Fast moving rivers

Fast-moving rivers require a slightly different approach from what we've covered so far.

Generally, anglers don't sit for hours at the side of a fast-moving river, they often move up and down the bank to where the fish are.

Let's look at how we might fish a fast-moving river. The main characteristics of fast-moving rivers are:

They're moving – fast

They're usually not deep

The colour of the water can change dramatically

The depth of the water can change dramatically

The river banks and the bottom are generally more uneven than a lake or a slow-moving river.

Selecting a swim is often easier on a river than it is elsewhere because of the features which make the swims more noticeable.

Look for weir pools which often attract fish waiting for food to spill over the edge.

Watch for fish moving on the surface or in the shallow waters, look for overhanging trees or for reed beds, or any other feature that might be used as shelter by fish.

Bends in the river create natural areas inside and outside the bend where fish might lurk.

The best way to fish a fast-moving river depends on the speed of the flow and of its width. For smaller rivers use a float. On slightly wider and deeper rivers, a feeder might be the best solution to present the bait.

QUOTE:

A bad day fishing is still better than a day in the office.

- *Anon*

ADVICE:

Check the speed of the flow for loosefeeding by chucking your bait into the flow about 10 or 12 feet before your hookbait, try to observe the speed at which the feed sinks – does it go near to your hookbait?

Practice the loosefeeding and understand what the feed is doing in the water.

ADVICE:

Choose flat feeders and leger weights to prevent your hookbait rolling away in the flow.

The flow creates a great opportunity to present the hookbait in a unique way.

By feeding the line from your reel, the speed of the float and the hookbait can be stopped at any point to stop it rolling any further.

When the flow is too strong, legering might be favourable if you can get your loosefeed close to the hookbait.

Depending on the speed of the flow and the fish likely to be present, choose your method, tactics and bait accordingly. Keep the loosefeed light, and let the fish find your swim. If you're failing to catch, go for lighter tackle – a size 16 or 18 hook, maybe.

Bait: Use maggots, worms, corn, bread, and pellets. Use deadbaits and lures for the predators.

Expect to catch: dace, grayling, chub, barbel, and occasionally pike, zander and eels.

Drains

Drains are man-made channels designed to drain the surrounding farmland. In the Fens, around the 17th century, the rise in agriculture frequently caused flooding and widespread devastation forcing landowners to act.

Drains were cut to ease the pressure on the rivers and provide additional drainage from the land.

Some of the larger drains were later occasionally used as canals to move crops and coal between towns and cities.

It is estimated that the drains still syphon around 10% of all UK floodwater away from the farmland around Lincolnshire, Cambridgeshire and Norfolk.

A **ADVICE:**

Never fish a drain unless you have permission from the farmer or a permit from the fishery or fishing club.

Many anglers dismiss drains due to their featureless appearance. But pre-baiting can concentrate the fish into a remote swim. Huge shoals of bream and roach have been reported.

Drains vary in width between 5ft and 100ft, and most have a depth between 1 and 4ft. Many drains are remote, and on private land, so access can be difficult or impossible.

Due to the remoteness of some drains, many remain unexplored and can provide excellent fishing opportunities, with most offering free fishing – check before you fish.

Let's look at how we might fish a drain. Drains are stillwaters but, depending on any recent rainfall, anglers can experience flow as the floodwaters drain to the sea.

Drains tend to be flat bottomed and almost completely featureless, save for the occasional bridge. Unlike canals, drains have no towpath (although most have a pathway close-by), so access to the bank could be tricky especially when the drain is in a steep-sided trench.

When selecting your swim, look for fish moving on the surface, and look for any feature that might be used as shelter by fish.

There is a range of ways to fish a drain, depending on the fish being targeted. Most people fish the drains for pike, perch, zander, eels and wels catfish. These are generally big hardy fish often caught on deadbaits or lures.

Use a stout rod, 15-20lb line, and a wire trace if pike or zander expected.

On the drains, where the water is clear, silver fish thrive.

Some drains bring reports of large catches of bream, tench and roach, even carp. The local angling clubs often control these drains.

Bait: Use maggots and worms for the silver fish, and deadbaits and lures for the predators.

Expect to catch: Roach and bream in some places, but many predators such as pike, perch, zander, eels and wels catfish.

FIVE Specialist fishing

I recognise this guide is intended for beginners but, for completeness, I've included a short chapter on specialist fishing - fishing for specimen fish, and fishing for predators with lures instead of a float or feeder.

I DO NOT recommend that beginners take-up specialist fishing; not until they've learnt to fish – to hook the fish, to use a landing net, to use a disgorger, to handle the fish correctly, and to return it safely to the water unharmed.

Barbel

Barbel is a fighting fish – possibly the hardest fighter of all freshwater fish. Strong tackle is needed to control its explosive bursts of power as it lunges towards the nearest sanctuary. In fast-moving water, Barbel thrive – close to weirs, on the outside of bends and around snags.

Any gravel-bottomed river is the ideal spot for Barbel; their mouths sift through the gravel to find food.

Barbel is often caught with a float in rivers, but the best method is feeder or leger. Loosefeed with hemp, and try sweetcorn, boilies, or meat as hookbait.

Loosefeed different size pellets, and fish with a pellet on the hook.

Carp

Try adding salt or chilli sauce to carp baits; the added flavour seems to work, especially on particle bait loosefeed.

Carp is a big, strong fish; strong tackle is needed to fight them as they race away from you.

Carp are caught on float or feeder. The feeder is the preferred method, with a range of variations on the conventional method being used with great success.

Walk into any fishing tackle shop, and you'll be amazed at the vast range of tackle – especially the rig-building components.

Carp like islands, gravel banks, overhanging trees and other features. Casting into those areas must be accurate; carp anglers go to great lengths to prepare their equipment before fishing.

Carp love to feed at night, so some fishing sessions last from one day to the next. Carp anglers either must be nocturnal or light sleepers.

The favoured baits are sweetcorn, bread, pellets or boilies.

Zander, Pike and Wels Catfish

IMPORTANT:

Many fisheries have banned live baits – check before you fish.

Zander, Pike and Wels Catfish are predators – they feed on anything that moves in the water, including their own young. They are caught on most dead or live baits. The deadbaits can include sea fish and freshwater fish. The preferred method for livebaiting is float fishing so the fish may move around. Float fishing can also be used for deadbaits. Larger specimens tend to be caught on legered dead baits.

Due to the size and strength of the predators, strong tackle is required, including wire traces to prevent the fish from biting through the line.

An alternative fishing method for zander and pike, and large perch, is spinning – this is covered next.

Spinning

Spinning is an alternative to float fishing or legering; it entails pulling an artificial lure through the water to attract predator fish such as pike, zander and large perch, and the occasional chub.

The lures, typically, take on the appearance of small fish.

Lures can be categorised as spinners, spoons, plugs, jiggers, flies, soft lures, and so on. There is no clear definition of each type.

The method is uncomplicated, and rarely requires seats, brollies, loads of bait, and so on – spinning is often about roaming the water looking for signs of fish, casting the lure into a swim in different places hoping to attract the fish, coaxing them out of the hiding places.

Spinning rods are shorter and lighter than float or feeder rods.

Fixed-spool reels are used, as are swivels for bait presentation, and wire traces to prevent the line being cut by the teeth of the predators.

By casting to the shadows of trees, boats or other features, the angler can often find fish that lie in wait for their prey.

Don't ignore the near margins and the water directly in front of you.

The predators tend to wait in the margins, in the shadows waiting for their unsuspecting prey.

When spinning, the angler often covers all the water by casting in a fan pattern.

The approach ensures all the water is covered in a methodological manner – see the diagram over the page.

Try to avoid pointing the rod towards the lure; this prevents line breakages as a fish takes the bait. Always keep the rod at 90 degrees to the line.

GOING FISHING

Drop-shotting

Drop-shotting is a variation on spinning; it entails pulling an artificial lure through the water to attract predator fish such as pike, zander and large perch.

The lures can be any natural bait such as worms or maggots, or artificial baits that take on the appearance of small fish.

The method is uncomplicated and is often about roaming the water looking for signs of fish, casting the lure into a swim in different places hoping to attract the fish, coaxing them out of the hiding places.

Drop-shotting rods are shorter and lighter than float or feeder rods. Fixed-spool reels are used, as are swivels for bait presentation.

The drop-shot method is like deep sea fishing, where the weight is on the end of the line, and the hook is above it. By putting the bait into a flow or creating the flow by pulling the bait through the water, the bait becomes attractive.

Drop-shotting, or finesse fishing, has been a popular method in the US for many years, where the bait is often presented from a boat.

GOING FISHING

SIX It's time to go fishing

The time has finally come for you to make the first fishing trip but, before you head off, there are a few final preparations to make.

Weather

This may seem obvious, what's the weather forecast?

Make sure you're prepared for the weather – whatever it is.

Experience says that sat on the edge of a lake, or on a river bank; you will be exposed to the harshest conditions – there's no shelter from the wind on a 100-acre lake.

The sun will burn, the wind will blow your tackle away, the rain will sting as it hits you – be prepared or wait for another day.

I can't stress this enough; the weather can do harm and damage, so be ready for it.

Use a simple weather app on your phone to check the forecast, take waterproof clothing if rain is expected. DO NOT be complacent.

IMPORTANT:

As the glare of the sun reflects off the surface of the water, you will be exposed to a double dose of its rays – you could burn within minutes.

QUOTE:

To go fishing is one of the most pleasurable experiences I can imagine.

- *Fennel Hudson*

Permit - limitations and rules

Make sure you've got your licence and a permit. Read the permit, know and understand the rules and limitations.

I bagged-up with over 50 decent fish last week – 'no keepnets allowed' – each fish was returned as I unhooked it. Those were the rules. It would have been nice to see them in a keepnet though!

Interestingly, the popular fishery had been visited by the Environmental Agency inspectors the day before; 23 anglers were fishing – four had no licence.

How long?

The length of your fishing trip might dictate what other 'equipment' you might need. You've got your fishing tackle ready, but what about water, food, warm clothing, phone, charger, hat, glasses, medication, toilet roll, sunglasses, sun cream, and so on.

Think ahead; it's too late when you're already fishing and realise you left something behind.

Tackle

Don't try to carry every bit of fishing tackle you own. Consider what you might need – rods, reels, pole, nets, floats, feeders, hooks, line, disgorgers, plummets, and so on.

Make sure you've got it, it's clean, and it's working.

Check you know how the rod goes together, how to align the rod rings, and how to fit the reel. Make sure the reel handle is on the correct side of the reel, and that the reel spool is full of line.

Rigs

Don't wait until you get to the water before you build your rigs. If you can do this at home for pole or feeder fishing, then it saves time at the water's edge.

Make sure the rigs cover most combinations: line length, line thickness, hook size, etc. Label the rigs, so you know what they are: hook size, line length, and line breaking strain.

Tackle Box

Sort and pack everything you need into your tackle box.

Keep it neat and tidy; check that everything is labelled, especially hook sizes, and shot weights. Keep the essential items at the top your tackle box; bits such as disgorgers and plummets will need to be easily accessible.

Bait

Don't make the mistake of buying your bait on the way to your fishing spot. Sod's Law says the shop will be shut, or they will have no bait – buy it beforehand.

Check the bait before you leave home to make sure it's still fresh and usable.

Final Preparations

Have you forgotten something? The answer is probably, yes!

IMPORTANT:

Tell someone where you're going. Don't let people worry if they're trying to contact you but can't get a mobile phone signal.

GOING FISHING

SEVEN | Going Fishing!

This is where the research, planning, preparation, and theory, come together; these are exciting times.

DO NOT rush to get set up; follow the simple steps set out in this section. Above all, take your time and enjoy the experience.

Watch

As you approach the water and get close to your swim, try to keep a low profile, keep the noise down, and avoid stomping around and dropping things.

Shadows on the water and noise or vibration on the bank will spook the fish – it's pointless ruining a day's fishing before you've started.

Stay back from the water's edge and watch for signs of fish: bubbles, rolling and splashing, all visible on the surface.

When you think you're in the right place, and you feel confident that you're ready to catch the fish, it's time to get your tackle together.

A ADVICE:

Don't be in a hurry to start fishing; take your time to look around you. There's no point in setting-up a loaded waggler to fish 30 yards out when the fish are under your rod tip.

Peg set up

It's important to set up your peg neatly and efficiently. This avoids your tackle being spilt, lost, and broken.

If you intend to fish in the same place for a while, start by positioning your seat - ensuring it's close enough to reach the water but far enough away from the edge to stand without falling in.

I set my seat about 2-3ft from the edge of the bank; this allows me to stretch my legs.

Match anglers, with their 'fishing platform' seat boxes, generally prefer to sit right on the edge of the water – it takes much practice.

If you want to enjoy your fishing experience, make yourself comfortable and don't perch on the edge.

With your seat in place, have a good look round for obstacles that might snag or break your tackle, check for footpaths where people must get past you – don't block their route.

One way to avoid broken tackle is to keep everything off the ground, especially your fishing rod or pole.

So, start by putting rod rests in place; if you're float fishing with a rod, position one rest about 3-4ft in front of you (at the water's edge) and one at the side of your seat.

With your rod rests (or pole rests) set up, use them.

Make sure your landing net is close to hand; assemble it before you start fishing.

Likewise, bait boxes need to be near to you so that you can quickly grab the loosefeed, groundbait and hookbait. Position the bait boxes so the bait can't be spilt.

A ADVICE:

I have a seat box attachment that's a rod rest – it's a great little device, and it saves so much time – I just hook it on.

Tackle set up

Rod and float

If you've decided to fish with a float and rod, take your rod from its bag and assemble the rod, making sure the joints are clean before pushing them together.

Align the rod rings by sighting down the rod and twisting the rod sections, then push together to secure each joint.

Take your reel from its bag and connect it to the rod using the reel seat; ensure the reel is aligned with the rings on the rod, then secure the reel.

Place the rod in the rod rests.

At this point, I would gather the tackle I will need: float, float stoppers, hook (or hooklink), and shot.

By following this sequence, assemble the tackle to the line:

> Open the bail arm of the reel, take the end of the line directly from the spool and thread the line through the rod rings.

> Then pull the end of the line towards the handle of the rod and close the bail arm by rotating the reel handle one turn, making sure the end of the line is roughly in line with the reel.

The rest of this sequence can be completed while you sit on your seat:

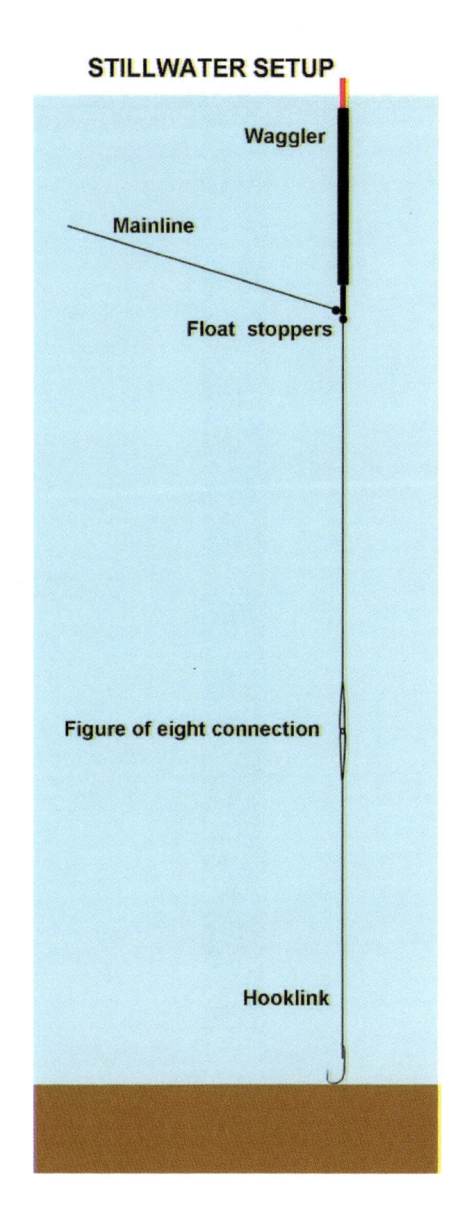

> With a tight line, attach a float stopper then your chosen float and a second float stopper. Push the float and float stopper assembly together.

> Slide the assembly about 3ft up the line towards the rod tip.

> Practice tying the simple knots at home, until you get good at tying each one; it's much more difficult trying to tie knots at the water.

Then, either:

    Tie the hook to the line using one of the prescribed knots.

Or

    Connect the hooklink to the line by creating a 1in loop at the end of the line using a figure of eight knot - trim the excess line.

    Use a simple figure of eight loop to connect the hooklink.

Secure the hook around part of the reel seat or the first ring, gently tighten the line by turning the reel handle and setting the anti-reverse.

You're now ready to check the depth and set your float. It's best to do this before adding shot to the line, so a true indication of the depth is obtained – see the next section on plumbing the depth of water around your swim and setting the float.

Pole

For pole or whip fishing, the set-up procedure is much simpler; this sequence can be completed while you sit on your seat:

    Select the rig you will use and secure it to the connector at the tip.

    Carefully connect the joints (either push-together or telescopic) making sure the joints are clean before securing each one.

    Unwind the line from the pole winder simultaneously.

With the rig entirely unwound from the winder, you can either:

(With a take-apart pole) Secure the hook around the end of the pole sections.

Alternatively:

(With a telescopic pole) Secure the hook around a tightly-wound rubber band fastened around the pole.

You're now ready to check the depth and set your float.

Rod and feeder

Having decided to fish with a feeder, take your rod from its bag and assemble the rod, making sure the joints are clean before pushing them together. Align the rod rings by sighting down the rod and twisting the rod sections, then push together to secure each joint.

Take your reel from its bag and connect to the rod using the reel seat; ensure the reel is aligned with the rings on the rod, then secure the reel.

Place the rod in the rod rests.

At this point, I would gather the tackle I'm going to need: feeder, stopper, and hook (or hooklink). By following this sequence, assemble the tackle to the line:

Open the bail arm of the reel, take the end of the line directly from the spool and thread the line through the rod rings.

Then pull the end of the line towards the handle of the rod and close the bail arm by rotating the reel handle one turn, making sure the end of the line is roughly in line with the reel.

The rest of this sequence can be completed while you sit on your seat.

Slide a barrel swivel and a leger stop onto the mainline.

Connect the hooklink to the end of the mainline using a simple figure-of-eight loop.

Approximately 15in from the hook fix the leger stop (or small shot).

Attach a feeder with around 12in of line to the swivel by using one of the prescribed knots.

Secure the hook around part of the reel seat or first ring, gently tighten the line by turning the handle of the reel and engaging the anti-reverse.

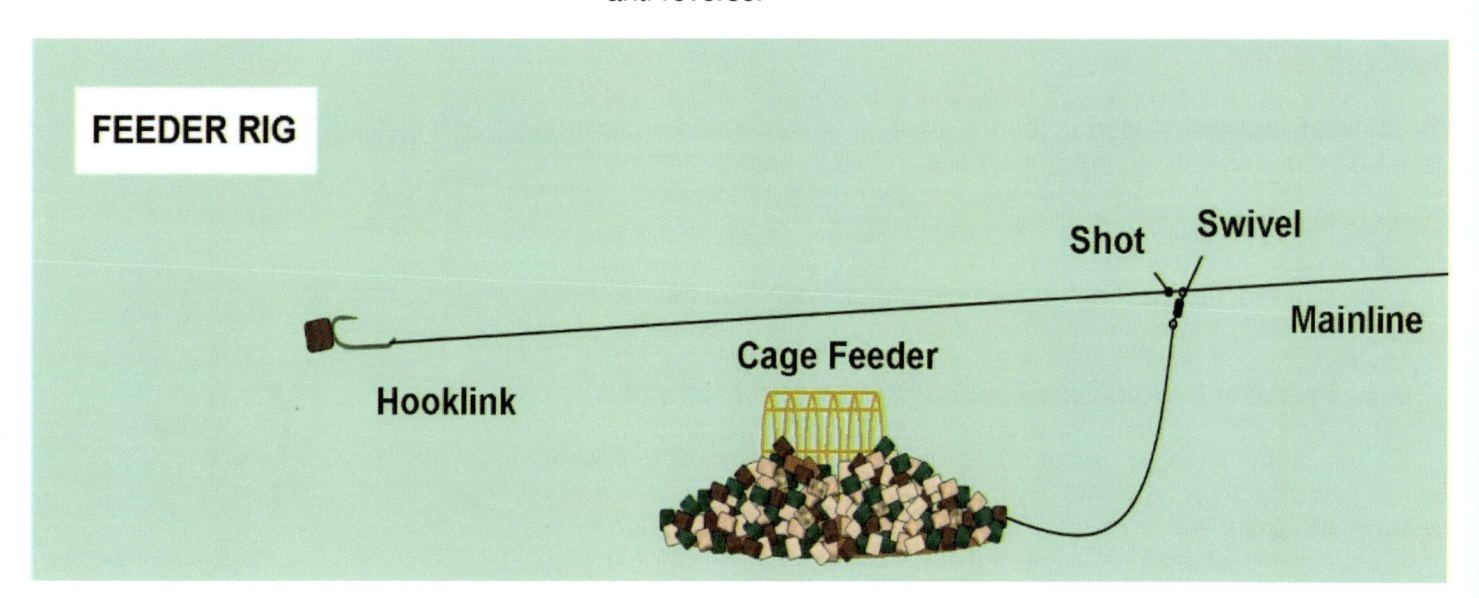

FEEDER RIG

Hooklink — Cage Feeder — Shot — Swivel — Mainline

In the diagram, we show a cage feeder, but the rig could be used with any type of feeder. Note that Method feeders are connected to the mainline, and the hooklink is connected directly to the Feeder.

You're almost ready to fish.

Check depths

For float fishing, you probably want to set the hook to sit almost at the bottom of the lake, canal or slow-moving river.

By plumbing the water in many places around your 'swim', you develop an impression of the shape of the bottom – any ledges, troughs, and so on.

Don't rush when checking the depth; time taken to plumb the depth often dictates the number of fish caught.

MORE TIME = MORE FISH

Rod anglers

If you're using a rod:

> Fasten the plummet to your hook, pull back the bail arm on your reel, and toss the plummet into the water.
>
> WAIT!
>
> Look for the float coming to the surface, making sure there is no tension in the line. If the float doesn't appear, it means you will be fishing too shallow. Gently put tension in the line by turning the reel handle and, lift the tip of the rod to pull the plummet about 1ft towards you. WAIT!
>
> Again, look for the float coming to the surface, making sure there is no tension in the line. If the float doesn't appear, it means you will be fishing too shallow. Gently lift the tip of the rod to pull the plummet about 1ft towards you.
>
> WAIT!

Keep repeating this process until the tip of the float appears. If you want to fish further out into the water, set the float about a foot deeper (by moving it further from the hook). Then go back to step one.

GOING FISHING

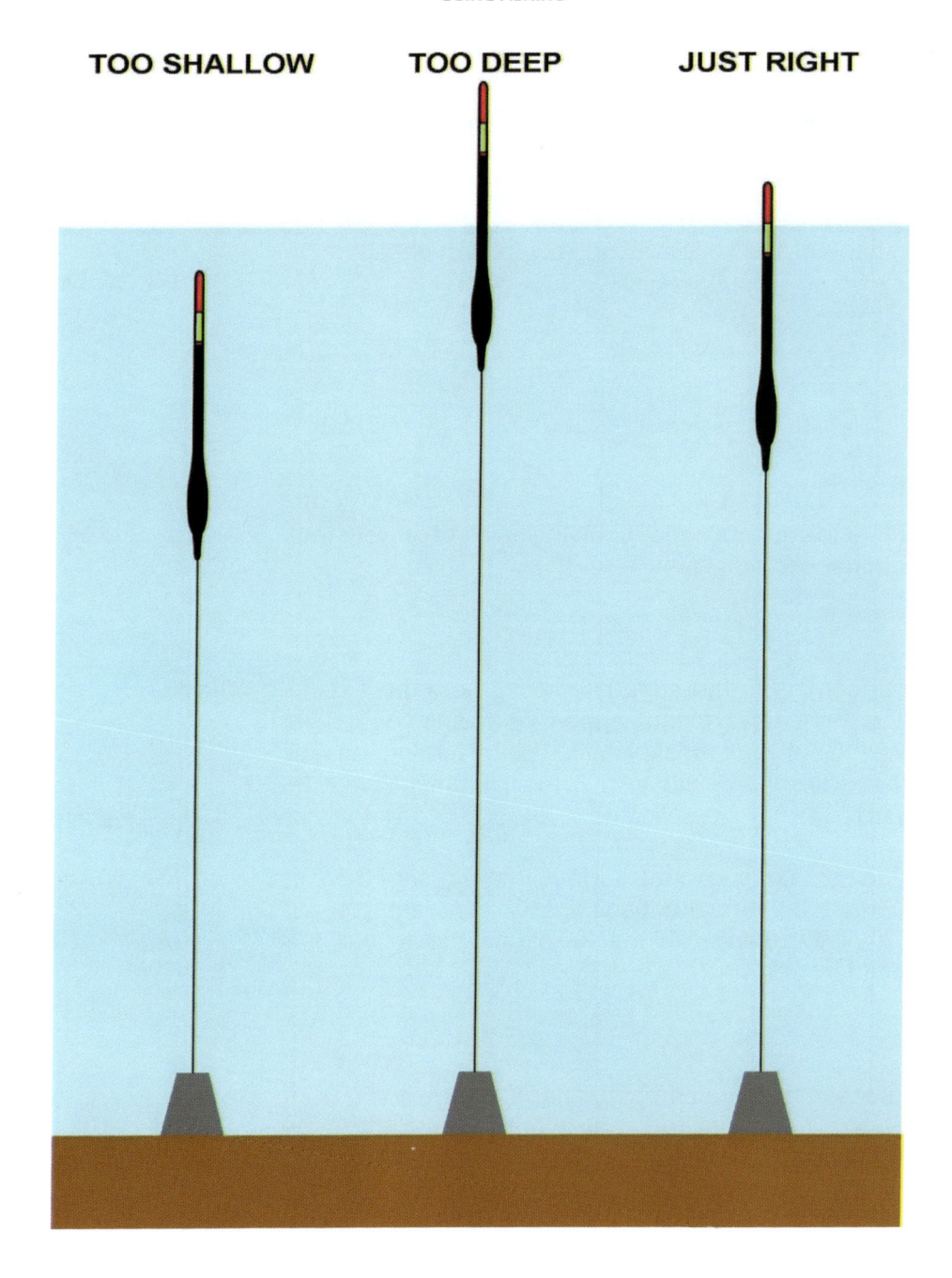

TOO SHALLOW **TOO DEEP** **JUST RIGHT**

PAGE 88

If the float is on the surface but doesn't sit correctly (vertically, with only the tip showing), then you will be fishing too deep. In which case, move the float nearer to the hook.

It could take a few minutes for you to build up a picture of the depth of your swim – but it is time well spent.

If you want to fish a long way out (further than you can safely toss the plummet), then you must cast the plummet into the water; we cover casting in the next section.

Use a plummet that allows the hook to touch the bottom of the water. Some plummets attach to the hook, leaving the hook 1-2in above the bottom.

Pole anglers

For pole anglers, fasten the plummet to your hook, and lower the float into the water.

Watch for the float, move the plummet around your swim to build a picture of the depth. Set your float so that only the tip is visible.

It is advisable to use a heavy plummet so that you can feel the bottom of the water as you move the plummet around your swim.

Adding shot

With the float depth established, it's time to add weight to get the float sitting in the water correctly.

It's not just a matter of fixing a bunch of shot to the line, placing each shot is important.

Different fish feed at different levels in the water. Roach and bream, for example, feed on the bottom, some other fish feed higher in the water.

The presentation of the hookbait depends on the pattern of shot.

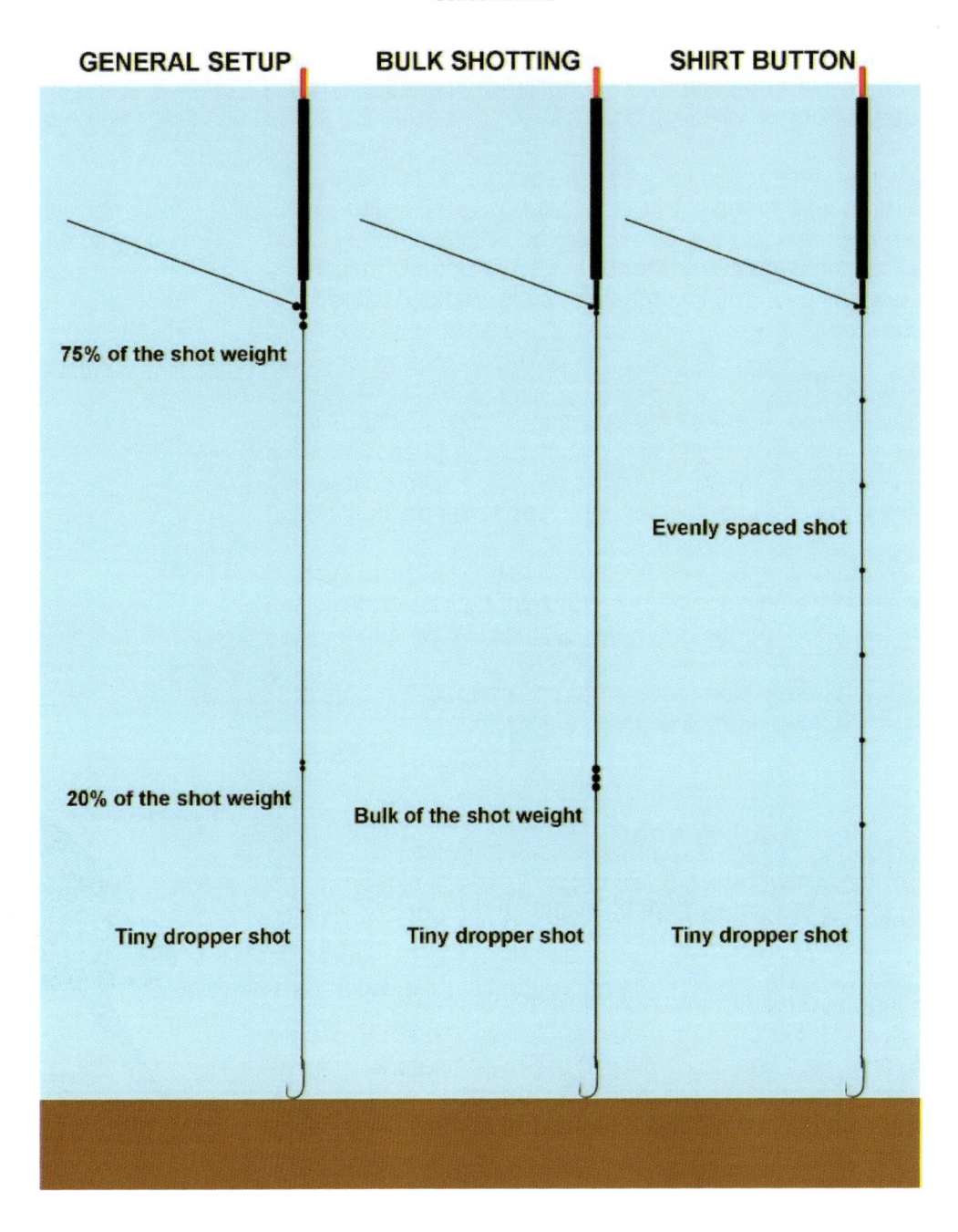

GENERAL SETUP

75% of the shot weight

20% of the shot weight

Tiny dropper shot

BULK SHOTTING

Bulk of the shot weight

Tiny dropper shot

SHIRT BUTTON

Evenly spaced shot

Tiny dropper shot

If the fish are higher in the water, it's no good racing through them with the bait; it's better to let the bait fall more slowly.

To give the fish a chance to grab the bait as it gently sinks, you place most of the shot weight towards the float with smaller shot down the line.

The general setup is where most of the weight (around 75%) is placed directly below the float. A further 20% of the weight is placed about a third of the distance from the hook to the float. The remaining weight, the dropper shot, is placed about 6in from the hook.

To catch roach, you need your bait to go straight to the fish, in which case you place most of the weight towards the hook – the bait will immediately sink to where the fish are. This a called bulk shotting.

The bulk shotting method gets the hookbait to the fish quickly.

By equally spacing the weight in a shirt button pattern, the bait sinks more naturally.

The tiny dropper shot is used to let the hook bait settle gently into place. It also helps to register lift bites without spooking the fish.

Some anglers use a combination of these methods by, for example, combining the general setup with the shirt button pattern.

In which case, the bulk of the shot is placed around the float, with the remaining weight being added as small shot spaced 1-2in apart above the dropper shot.

I mostly use the general setup, but if I sense bites on the drop, I might move the shot up the line.

But if I'm being pestered by small fish on the surface, I might move the shot down the line.

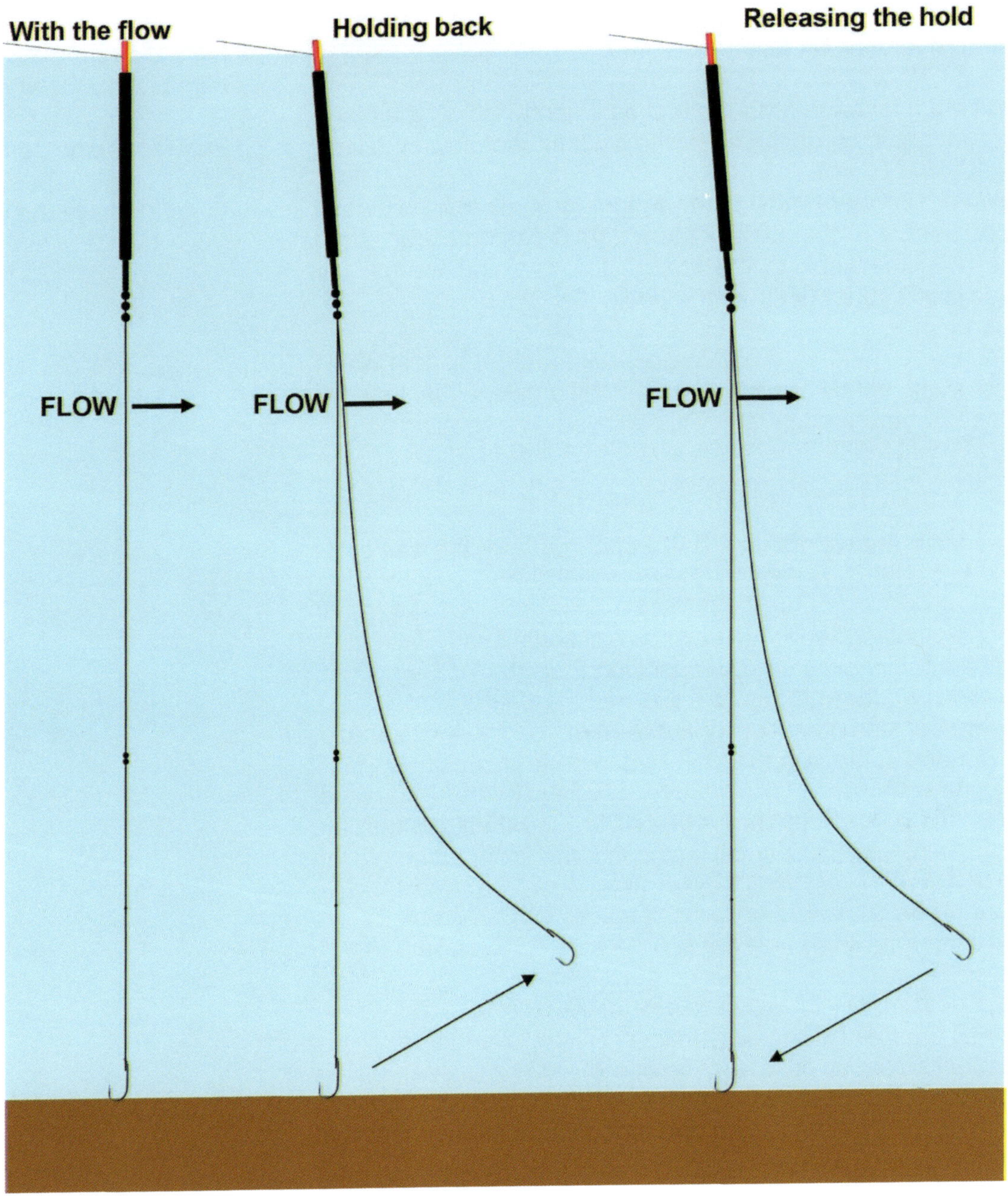
With the flow
Holding back
Releasing the hold
FLOW
FLOW
FLOW

For rivers, the shot pattern has a greater effect on the natural presentation of the bait.

The flow of the river creates a buoyancy in the line; it's never going to be vertical, so you decide how the flow will affect the bait and how you want to present the bait to the fish.

Trotting the bait with the flow, allows the fish to see the bait as it moves with the current.

In faster moving rivers, it's often useful to slow the trot slightly and move at around half the pace of the normal flow.

As you hold the float back, the line will move forward forcing the bait off the bottom. It is imperative that the float is shotted correctly to allow the bait to be presented according to the fish and the flow.

To keep the bait towards the bottom use bulk shot towards the hook, shirt-buttoning will keep the bait higher in the water and, depending on the flow and the bait; a general setup will allow the bait to rise even higher in the water.

Some anglers use the flow to cause the bait to rise and fall which allows the bait to be presented at different levels.

By holding back the float, the bait rises, and by releasing the float, the bait drops back to the bottom.

QUOTE:

There's fishing a... looking like an...

- Anon

Casting

Casting is an essential skill for freshwater anglers; getting the hookbait into the right place is paramount to catching fish.

Here we go through the stages of casting with a fixed spool reel (I would recommend that you do this while standing until you get the hang of it).

GOING FISHING

...d recommend that you
...to cast without a hook or a
...; maybe start with a small
...er weight on a large lake with
...othing to hamper your cast.

You will soon get the hang of it.

Before you cast, check behind and above for any obstacles that might hinder your cast and spoil your day:

Hold your rod in your chosen (or dominant) hand with your fingers wrapped around the reel seat.

Lift the tip of the rod to 45 degrees (halfway between horizontal and vertical) in front of you.

Turn the handle on your reel to place your hook about 4-5ft above the ground level.

Turn the spool of the reel so that your finger is next to the line roller.

Holding the line with your forefinger, disengage the bail arm of the reel.

With your other hand on the butt end of the rod (don't move this hand), slowly rotate the rod vertically around the butt end so that it's 45 degrees behind you.

Take care not to tangle the line and tackle around your rod as you reach the near-vertical position – move the tip of the rod slightly to one side to allow the line and hook to pass the rod.

We want to get the weight moving forward and creating enough momentum to pull line from the reel (it takes little effort).

We started in position 1 and rotated the rod back to position 6 now we need to get back to position 1. Before we do that, note where position 3 is. Position 3 is now the most important position

So, rotate the rod forward purposefully to position 1, but just before position 3 release the line (you should feel the line pull when you need to release it). Lower the rod tip as the bait touches the water.

The cast needs to be smooth and purposeful.

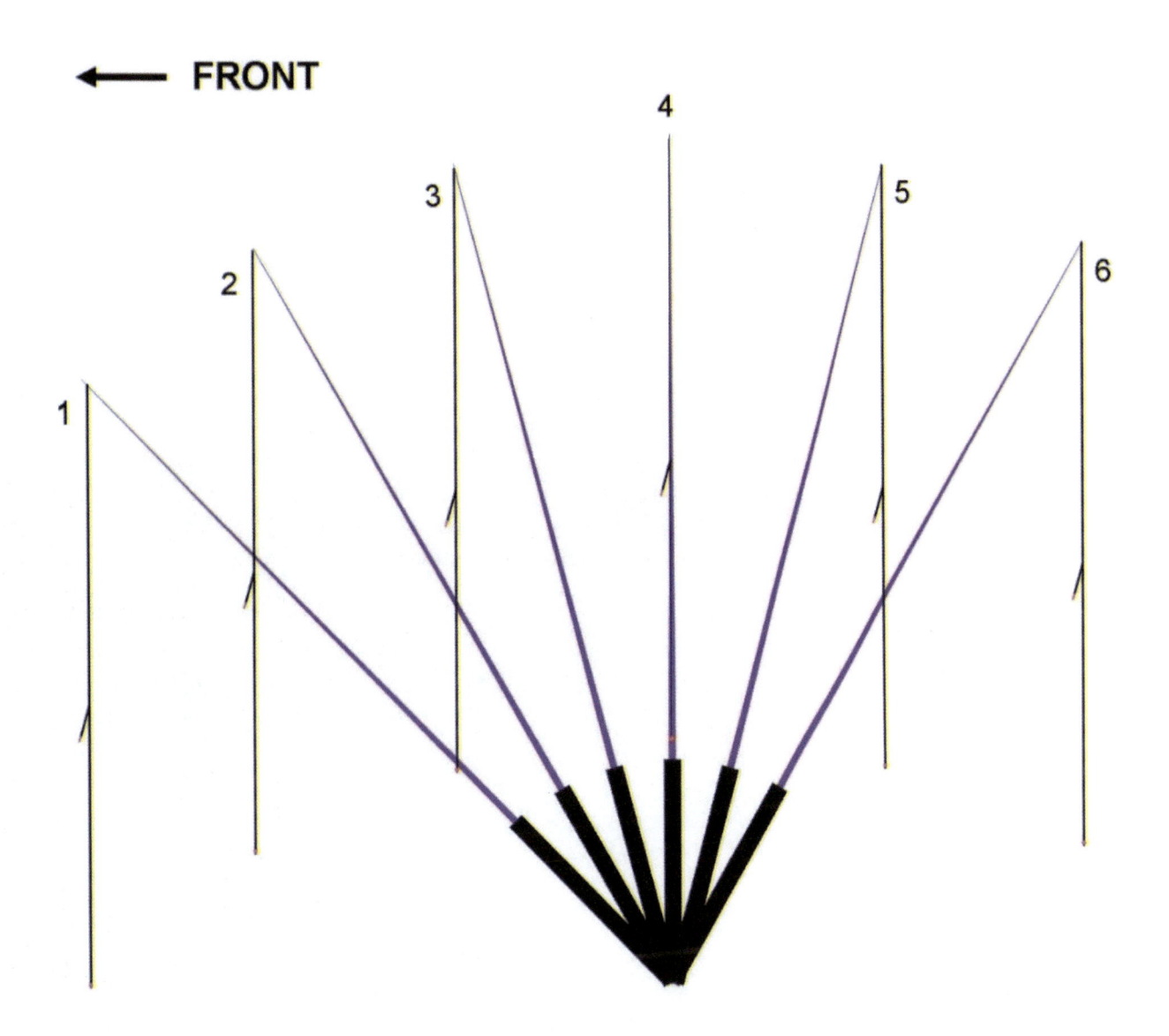

With the cast completed, tighten the line to maintain contact with the hookbait.

> **QUOTE:**
>
> The best times to fish are when it's raining and when it isn't.
>
> *- Patrick F McManus*

Distance and direction

It's important to fish the part of your swim that contains the groundbait and loosefeed. Try to avoid casting randomly and then adding feed wherever the float or feeder lands.

Accuracy in casting depends on two things - distance and direction. However, faced with an open stretch of water, both can be difficult to achieve unless you're using a pole.

Let's explore casting distance first

You might have noticed a small clip on the side of the spool of your reel – the line clip. As a beginner, I will explain how to fish at the same distance every cast. This works for both floats and feeders.

Simply, cast your bait into the area you want to fish and, with the bail arm off, raise your rod to around 45 degrees to release another 4-5ft of line. Wrap the line from your spool around the line clip and wind your reel to set the bail arm.

Reel in.

OK, now cast your bait into the same place, but keep your rod raised at 45 degrees to absorb some of the shock of the momentum. Your line clip will stop the bait at the distance you set. Try not to cast further. Otherwise, your line may break as the line stops and the weight continues.

As the bait is settling, wind in a half dozen turns to compensate for the 4-5 ft of line we released.

With a little practice, you will be fishing the same distance consistently.

Casting direction is slightly easier

Part of the key to consistent direction is casting accuracy; the other is knowing what direction to go.

The trick is not only to aim at a target in the distance (see diagram below) – a tree, a house, or pylon – but to also aim at a target in the water – a reflection. This is especially useful for float fishing in still water – where possible, establish a target in the reflection on the surface of the water and keep your hookbait, groundbait and loosefeed in that area.

I often see beginners casting with one hand, by letting go of the reel during the cast.

By taking their dominant hand off the rod, they lose their grip, control, and direction.

Casting accuracy takes a little practice, so take your time and reap the rewards.

> Try using bait additives by adding a small amount of the liquid to the loosefeed or groundbait. Additives, such as Hemp oil, will attract fish.

Loosefeeding

Once you're fishing, keep the loosefeed flowing – little and often. DO NOT overfeed the fish; just a few tempters to attract the fish, keep them interested, and encourage them to take your hookbait.

The accuracy of feed placement is important, make sure that it's aimed at your hookbait. Use a catapult, or throwing stick, if needed. Both devices need a little practice, but it pays dividends.

If you're fishing with a pole, small pole pots can be a great investment. They simply clip to the end of the pole, and loosefeed you put into the pot is tipped into the swim in exactly the right place. It's worth repeating what I said earlier about the loosefeed to use - I avoid using the hookbait as a loosefeed – in my view, large loosefeed makes my hookbait indistinguishable. I want my hookbait to stand out, so I normally use smaller bait samples for loosefeeding.

Patience

Being realistic, you will not catch loads of fish on your first trip – do not read through the angling press or watch the 'entertaining' angling shows on TV and set yourself an unrealistic expectation. Be patient!

Try to think like a fish: What's the weather doing? What colour is the water? How fast is the water flowing? How hungry am I? How much food is available? And so on. Warm weather might encourage fish to feed and to move up in the water. Cold weather might make fish sluggish and force them to stay low in the water.

Don't go chasing after every splash you see; encourage the fish to come to you – loosefeed, little and often.

Also, change your hookbait regularly; there are no rules on this, but I change my hookbait every few minutes, depending on the bait and method I'm using.

Experiment

When the fishing is slow, it's a good time to experiment. Don't hesitate to learn and try different methods – a pole instead of a rod, or a feeder instead of a float. It's also a good time to try new baits from the vast range that's available.

However, some experimentation might not be so radical. Instead of fishing in front of your peg, why not try the margins – fish can sometimes take shelter there? Alternatively, on a canal, why not try the near shelf (under your rod tip) instead of fishing the far shelf?

Never stop trying new things!

BITE!

It's hard to explain the excitement of the bite; for me it's amazing. It confirms that the research and preparation, and the learning, was all worthwhile. But, hey! The fish hasn't been caught yet. Let's talk about bites.

Bites come in all shapes and sizes, depending on the fish, the bait and the method. For carp anglers, fishing the method, the bite is often announced by the bite alarm and line peeling off the reel.

For anglers fishing the float, the bite can show in various ways:

- The shy bite indicated by several slight dips in the float before it slides underwater
- The snatch indicated by the float simply going underwater
- The lift, where the float rises instead of going down
- The hesitant snatch, where the float twitches before going underwater.

Get to know the different types of bite, and try to anticipate each one. Some bites won't be obvious, so watch the movement of your float or rod tip and try to picture what's happening around your hook.

For feeder fishing, the bite can also show in different ways, often just like float fishing:

> The shy bite indicated by several slight tugs on the tip before it pulls to one side
>
> The snatch indicated by the tip pulling round
>
> The lift, where the tip goes loose instead of pulling forward
>
> The hesitant snatch, where the tip twitches before pulling round

Look for these and more, and enjoy every one!

Strike

The strike is the movement of the rod or pole that tightens the line and hooks the fish.

The strike isn't a slow action, nor is it a rapid action – it's a firm, deliberate action to hook the fish.

We don't want to hurt the fish, nor to lose the fish, we just want to hook the fish in the lip.

The strike depends on many factors, the type of water (river, lake, canal, etc.), the method of fishing, the fish being caught, the tackle and hookbait being used, and the distance between the rod/pole tip and the hook. The bites also must be considered; is it a quick pull and release, is it a slow pull to one side, or is it a lift bite (where the float moves up instead of down)?

Striking cannot be oversimplified—it is an art form—to be perfected over many years. Top matchmen continually debate the different types of striking to a level I fail to understand.

We simply strike to hook the fish.

Try to avoid striking at every movement of your float or rod tip. Be sure that the fish has taken the hookbait, but don't wait until it spits out (or swallows) the hook.

For smaller fish, when using a pole, the strike is fast and purposeful, just like the bites. The distance from the pole tip to the hook is short and direct, so there is often no need to move the pole more than a foot or so.

Feeder fishing for carp over a long distance is a whole different matter. The strike must be firm and positive; feel for the fish and keep up the pressure.

At a local fishery, on a recent visit, I connected with a shoal of bream (mostly around 2-3lb) while fishing a short (5m) whip. Every bite made the float slide gracefully under the water; my strike was a lift of only a few inches. Easy; I lost only one fish all day.

Striking takes a lot of practice; sometimes you will miss many bites and wonder why. Think about the fish, the size of the bait, the hook size, and so on. Watch other anglers and continue to learn the art of striking.

Use the bend in the rod

Your fishing rod (or pole) is flexible; you've probably noticed a whip-like action, especially nearer the tip. That flex provides the power to fight the fish.

Let me explain; once the fish is hooked, it will fight (some more than others). Your hold on that fish relies upon the hook and the line, neither of those are flexible enough to absorb the bumps the fish produces as it fights. Imagine fighting a fish with a rod that is as inflexible as a broom handle – without the flexibility, it's an impossible job. The flexibility in the rod or pole provides the means to fight the fish.

Therefore, you must use the flexibility to its maximum effect to increase your chances of landing the fish.

The maximum power is achieved when the body of the rod is used at 90 degrees to the line. Simple!

Never point your rod or pole directly at the fish. Otherwise you will lose ALL the power to fight the fish. You will be relying on the flex in the line only.

DO NOT be afraid to let the fish fight – avoid rushing to get the fish into the net.

As you're playing the fish, always keep the main part of the rod or pole at 90 degrees to the line – watch the fish, watch the line, watch the rod, watch the angle.

After a while, it will become second nature, but for a beginner, not using the bend in the rod can lead to numerous broken lines and many lost fish.

Avoid the temptation to winch the fish towards you using the power of the reel. Let the bend in the rod do the hard work – use the reel to hold the line as the fish begins to tire.

With an elasticated pole, use the power of the elastic to fight the fish.

The elastic allows the pole to be stiffer which provides the ability to take on the bigger fish, such as carp.

Always match the pole elastic to the fish you're expecting to catch:

ELASTIC SIZE	TO CATCH
No 1 to No 4	Small silver fish
No 4 to No 6	Silver fish
No 8 to No 12	Carp and big silver fish
No 14 to No 18	Big carp in open water
No 20+	Big carp in the margins

A ADVICE:

I like to keep the handle of my rod or pole close to my forearm, especially when the fish is fighting. With my hand wrapped around the handle, I simply imagine that I'm pointing towards the fish – this helps maintain the 90-degree angle, which gives me maximum power from the rod.

Look after the fish - Return it unharmed

As you guide the fish towards the landing net, you're about to take on a responsibility to return that fish to the water unharmed. That is a big responsibility.

Any fish over 5 or 6in should be netted instead of being swung from the water. Once in the net, it should be lifted carefully from the water and not be allowed to bump into anything as your carry it to a safe place to be unhooked.

Don't try to scoop the fish from the water - glide the fish into the submerged net. Match anglers net the fish, unhook it while still in the net and release the fish into the keepnet within a second or two. We're not experienced match anglers; we're beginners, so we take our time to look after the fish.

If you want to weigh the fish, use a wet weigh sling and have the weighing equipment ready and waiting.

However, perhaps the matchmen can teach us something; depending on the design of your landing net, it can be the safe place to unhook the fish. If it's not, use a wet unhooking mat.

With the fish in a comfortable position, where it will not wriggle, jump or roll away, carefully remove the hook.

If the hook is deep, use a disgorger or a pair of forceps.

DO NOT leave the fish out of water for more than two minutes, keep the fish wet (so don't use fabric or gloves to hold the fish), and don't lift the fish too high above the ground in case you drop it.

Put the fish back into the water carefully. Don't drop the fishing into the water, hold it until it's strong enough to swim away.

Pack it neatly

Pack everything neatly – you'll thank yourself for it!

This is not going to be your last fishing trip; whatever sort of day you had today, you'll be back ready to catch more fish very soon.

So, as you're getting ready to go home, think about the next time you're going fishing, and consider how you want your equipment to be as you open each box, bag, holdall, etc.

Think about the kit you might need before your next trip, your bait boxes, for example. With this in mind, pack your fishing tackle and equipment neatly, in its right place, and accessible if you need it.

Remove any dirt or excessive water as you're packing the kit away.

Nothing is worse than getting to your peg on your next fishing trip and realising that you can't find your favourite float, your plummet, or your disgorger. Maybe your reel is clogged with dried mud or, worse still; there are dead and rotting maggots in your bait box.

Remove all litter

It is vitally important, for wildlife, and other anglers, that all litter is removed before you vacate your peg.

I always carry a plastic bag into which I put all litter, including bits of line, tackle, crisp packets, bottles (plastic), and leftover bait. I tie the bag as I'm leaving the peg and dump it into the bin when I get home.

Sadly, when I'm fishing, I often see discarded tackle, including line with shot and hooks, from other anglers.

It's not right! But, if you and I do the right thing, we'll help protect the wildlife from harm.

Happy Fishing!

GOING FISHING

Annex One

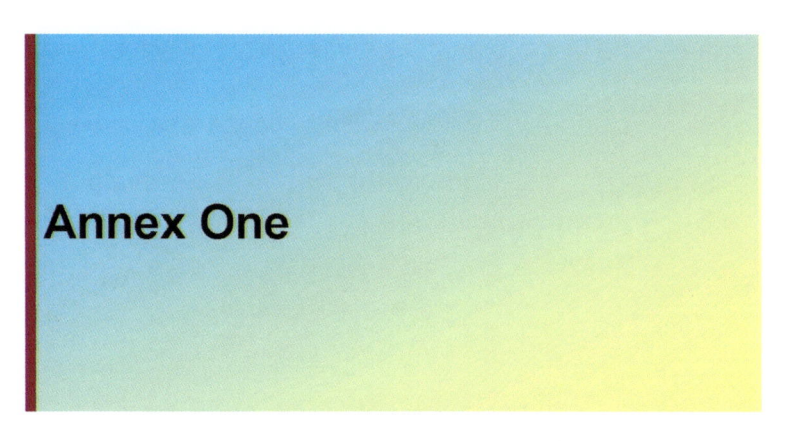

Weight Conversion

These weights are approximated; use them for guidance only.

Imperial (lb)	Metric (kg)	Metric (kg)	Imperial (lb)
0.062 (1oz)	0.028		
0.250 (4oz)	0.11		
0.50 (8oz)	0.22		
1.0	0.45	1.00	2.2
2.0	0.91	2.00	4.4
3.0	1.36	3.00	6.6
4.0	1.81	4.00	8.8
5.0	2.27	5.00	11.0
10.0	4.54	10.00	22.0
15.0	6.80	15.00	33.0
20.0	9.10	20.00	44.0
30.0	13.60		
40.0	18.20		
50.0	22.68		

For float shotting, it's best to know the weights and the equivalent shot sizes. These weights are approximated: use them for guidance only.

Shot Size	Shot Weight(g)	Equivalent
3SSG	4.8	6 x AAA
2SSG	3.2	4 x AAA
LG	3	
LSG	2	
SSG	1.6	2 x AA
AAA	0.8	2 x BB
AB	0.6	2 x No1
BB	0.4	2 x No4
No1	0.3	3 x No6
No3	0.25	2 x No6
No4	0.2	3 x No9
No5	0.15	2 x No8
No6	0.1	2 x No10
No8	0.06	2 x No11
No9	0.05	
No10	0.04	2 x No12
No11	0.03	3 x No13
No12	0.02	2 x No13
No13	0.01	

ANNEX ONE - CONVERSIONS

Length Conversion

These lengths are approximated; use them for guidance only.

Imperial (inches)	Metric (millimetres)
1	25
2	50
3	76
4	101
5	127
6	152
9	229
12	305

Imperial (feet & inches)	Metric (metres)
1	0.30
2	0.61
3	0.91
4	1.22
5	1.52
6	1.83
8	2.44
9	2.74
10	3.05
11	3.35
12	3.66
13	3.96
14	4.27

Annex Two

Typical Rules

These are 'typical' rules you **might** find on a permit.

1. Identity card to be carried at all times.
2. Fish to be returned alive to the water.
3. No gates to be left open.
4. No dogs.
5. No bonfires.
6. No night fishing.
7. Keepnets only to be used in matches.
8. Keepnets to be a minimum of 6ft 6in.
9. Minimum of 2 keepnets to be used: one for silver fish and one for carp only.
10. Maximum of 50lb in one keepnet.
11. No fish to be retained in keepnets for more than 6 hours.
12. All anglers should have a landing net, with a handle of at least 8ft.
13. Fish to be un-hooked in the landing net off the ground.
14. The use of padded unhooking mats is essential for specimen fish.

15. The following baits are banned: Bread, Boilies, Peanuts, Raisins, Pet Food, pellets, pellet paste, high protein groundbait, and other high protein bait, Bloodworms, Jokers, artificial baits, and floating baits.

16. 2 pint limit on Maggots and Casters, 1/2 kilo worms.

17. Groundbait limit 2kg.

18. All excess bait, containers and tackle should be taken home.

19. Any hook larger than a size 14 will be barbless.

20. Wire traces must be used at all times for pike fishing.

21. Only one rod to be used at any time.

22. Rods must not be left unattended.

Annex Three

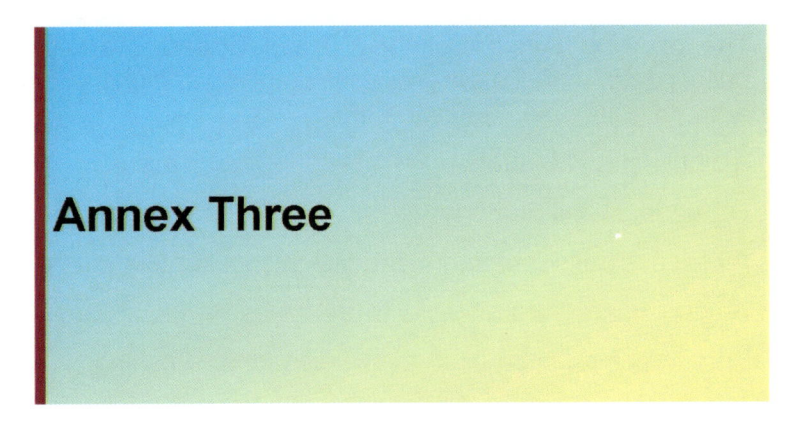

Interesting Rules

During our research on permits, we found some 'interesting' rules.

1. All types of audio equipment are banned.
2. You may trim any vegetation above the water's surface; please gather trimmed vegetation neatly on the bank.
3. Dip your boots before you fish.
4. No landing nets or keepnets, the fishery provides both.
5. No macaroni or pasta.
6. No floating pole, pole tapping or cupping of water.
7. No dead maggots.
8. When using bite alarms, keep the volume to a minimum.
9. The only pellets to be used are those that are purchased on site.
10. No candles.
11. No handling the fish with towels.
12. The use of elastic luggage straps is banned.

Annex Four

The Shopping List

Starting from scratch, this is a list of the kit you might need and an approximate price (at the time of publication). All the prices given here are for new tackle, albeit not the top of the range.

ITEM	ESSENTIAL	DESIRABLE	OPTIONAL
Licence (Year)	£30		
Seat box	£20		
Umbrella		£25	
Rod	£25		
Pole (11m)			£400
Whip (5m)		£15	
Reel	£15		
Line	£5		
Floats	£10		
Split shot	£2		
Leger weights		£3	
Feeders		£7	
Hooks	£2		

GOING FISHING

Disgorgers	£2		
Plummets	£2		
Float stops	£2		
Catapult	£5		
Tackle box	£10		
Landing net	£15		
Keepnet			£15
Banksticks (3)	£10		
Rod rests		£5	
Pole roller			£40
Bite alarm			£15
Bait boxes (3)	£5		
Holdalls	£20		
Trolley			£30
Bowls	£5		
Unhooking mat	£10		
	£200	**.. £50**	**£500**

So that's just £200 for a complete set of new fishing tackle you own, including the annual licence – just add a permit and some bait, and you're ready!

If you wanted to play golf instead, you're going to pay £550+ for clubs, shoes and silly trousers, then another £20 or more for your green fees; soon you'll realise you need lessons – that's another £20-30 for each lesson, and so it goes on.

The outlay for fishing tackle to get you started is great value and if you can buy used fishing stuff from an online outlet you might grab a real bargain – I've just seen 20 pole floats for £2.20 (that's just 11p each) .

Terminology

- A -

Action – the flexibility of a rod. Fast (or tip) action rods are stiffer but bend at the tip - often used in feeder fishing. Slow (or through) action rods are more flexible along their entire length - mainly used for float fishing.

Adjustable bankstick – bankstick with a sliding insert that allows you to change the length.

Anti-reverse – mechanism that prevents the spool of a reel from turning backwards.

Anti-tangle lead – running lead with silicone tubing either side of the weight reduce abrasion.

- B -

Back shot – small shot placed on the line above a float to help it remain steady in windy conditions.

Bail arm – part of a fixed-spool reel that guides the line onto the spool.

Bait – attractant for fish in the form of hookbait, groundbait, and loosefeed.

Bait band – small elastic band, wrapped around a bait, so the bait hangs from the bend of the hook.

Bait boat – remote controlled boat used to place rigs and loosefeed in remote swims.

Bait box – plastic box used for carrying bait.

Bait dropper – cage device used to drop groundbait into a swim – especially useful in rivers.

Bait needle – small hook for baiting hair rigs.

Bait rocket – rocket-shaped plastic tube filled with loosefeed and cast out into the swim – empties on impact with the water.

Balling up – throwing quantities of groundbait into a swim.

Bank – ground close to the water.

Bankstick – metal rod with a threaded end, to attach a rod rest, keepnet or bait alarm. The other end is pushed into the ground.

Barb – raised burr cut in a hook behind the point to stop the bait or fish coming off the hook.

Barbel – strong fighting fish, mainly found in fast-moving rivers.

Barbless hook – hook without a barb.

Bead – small plastic sphere with a hole through the centre. They can be used for buffering leads on rigs.

Berry – small edible fruit – can be used as hookbait.

Bite – indication that a fish has taken an interest in the hookbait.

Bite alarm – audible electronic device that detects line movement.

Bivvy – (Bivouac) – fabric shelter with a large opening to allow fishing from under it.

Blank – main part of a rod; has guides and a handle added to make the completed rod.

Blank – fishless day by the water.

Bleak – small silver fish.

Block end feeder – feeder with its ends covered, and a few holes around the body – mainly used for maggots.

TERMINOLOGY

Blood knot – type of knot commonly used for connecting two lines.

Bloodworm – small worm-like creature – can be used a hookbait.

Boilie – spherical bait, manufactured in various sizes, colours and flavours – can be used as hookbait or loosefeed.

Bolt rig – leger rig with a short hooklink; the fish feels the weight and 'bolts off', hooking itself.

Bowl – receptacle used to mix groundbait – usually made from flexible plastic.

Braid – strong woven fishing line of low diameter.

Brandling – red worm found in compost heaps – can be used as hookbait.

Bread – baked staple food – can be used as bait in various forms.

Bread crust – outer shell of a loaf of bread – can be used as hookbait.

Bread flake – softer inner 'meat' of a loaf of bread – can be used as hookbait.

Bread paste – bread flake mixed with water – can be used as hookbait.

Bread punch – implement with a circular 'punch' to create discs of bait, such as bread.

Breaking strain – measurement of line strength.

Bream – deep bodied fish often found in stillwaters.

Bumping off – losing a fish during a fight due to the hook coming loose.

Brolly – umbrella.

Bulk shot – closely-placed group of shot.

Butt – end of the rod nearest the angler.

- C -

Cage feeder – feeder comprising a wire mesh tube.

Cammo lead – weight with a painted cover that helps to blend into the background.

Carp – large stillwater fish.

Carp sack – bag designed to hold a carp in the water in place of a keepnet.

Carp sling – sling used for weighing carp and other large fish.

Cast – propelling the hookbait into the swim.

Caster – orange/red chrysalis of a maggot – can be used as hookbait and loosefeed.

Catapult – elasticated slingshot, used to throw loosefeed or groundbait.

Centrepin reel – free running reel mainly used for trotting.

Chinagraph pencil – hard wax pencil used to mark the fishing depth on a rod or pole.

Chub – fast cylindrical fish, commonly found in rivers.

Coarse fish – freshwater fish other than Salmon and Trout.

Cocktail – two types of bait on the hook at the same time.

Composite – two or more materials combined to make a rod or pole.

Corn – sweetcorn, often processed – can be used as hookbait or loosefeed.

Crucian Carp – small member of the carp family – mainly found in stillwaters.

Crystal waggler – waggler made of transparent plastic.

TERMINOLOGY

- D -

Dace – small, slender silver and red fish – often found in fast flowing rivers.

Deadbait – dead fish (or parts of fish) used as hookbait.

Diamond eye threader – thin wire, shaped as a four-sided diamond, used to thread elastic through the top section of a pole.

Disgorger – devices for removing hooks from fish.

Drag – feature on fishing reels that allows line to feed out.

Drain – man-made channels designed to drain the surrounding farmland.

Dropshot – method of fishing involving a lure, which is fished above a weight.

- E -

Eel – snake-like fish.

Elastic – extension to the line, housed inside the top section of a pole tip to help control fish when fighting.

Eye – small round hole at the end of a hook to tie the line to.

- F -

Feather the line – act of slowing the line to stop it spilling from the spool too quickly.

Feeder – a leger weight which carries groundbait or loosefeed.

Fibreglass – material used to make rods and poles.

Figure of Eight – simple knot, used to connect tackle to the line.

Fixed rig – leger rig where the weight is directly attached to the hook. Banned on most fisheries.

Fixed spool reel – fishing reel with a static spool; line is laid onto the spool by a rotating guide (bail arm).

Float – buoyant device used for hookbait presentation and bite detection.

Float fishing – use of floats to catch fish.

Float rod –light rod with a soft or an all-through action.

Float stop – small rubber/plastic device used to prevent the float sliding on the line.

Float tip – top-most part of a float, painted with a highly visible paint.

Fluorocarbon – fishing line that's virtually invisible underwater.

Forceps – long thin pliers, used to remove hooks.

- G -

Gap (or gape) – the distance between the shank of a hook and the point.

Gear – another term for fishing tackle and equipment.

Goundbait – powdered bait, used wet to attract fish to a swim.

Gozzer – home-bred maggot.

Grayling – streamlined silver fish often found in fast-moving water.

Grinner – reliable, strong knot.

Gudgeon – tiny elongated fish, found in fast-moving rivers.

Guide – ring on a rod used to guide the line.

TERMINOLOGY

- H -

Hair rig – short, thin section of line hanging from the back or bottom of the hook, which attaches to the bait.

Hair stop – small plastic device to keep boilies on the hair rig.

Half blood knot – reliable knot used for connecting tackle.

Hempseed – small black particle – can be used as hookbait or loosefeed.

Holdall – bag for carrying tackle.

Hook – sharp bent metal device used to catch fish.

Hookbait – bait used on the hook.

Hooklength – length of line attached to the hook.

Hook tyer – device to help tie hooks directly to the line.

- I -

In-line feeder – feeder rig comprising a main line running through the feeder.

In-line leads – leger rig comprising a main line running through the weight.

Insert waggler – float with a thin insert in the top to increase sensitivity.

- J -

Joker – small larva of a midge – can be used as loosefeed.

- K -

Keepnet – knotless tubular net designed to hold fish until the end of the session.

- L -

Landing net – net used to lift a fish from the water without harm; comprises a handle and a head (net).

Lateral line – visible line on the side fish indicating the sensory organs.

Lead – term referring to a weight, especially a weight for legering.

Lead bomb – tear-shaped lead with a swivel at the pointed end.

Leger (a.k.a. ledger) – method of fishing without a float with the bait anchored to the bottom of the water by a lead.

Leger rig – tackle comprising lead, hook (or hooklength), mainline and a connector – used for legering.

Leger stop – small plastic ring and plug to stop the lead sliding down the line.

Leger weight – a weight used for legering, typically a lead bomb.

Licence – in the UK, all anglers over 12 years old need a Licence from the Environmental Agency.

Line – fine cord used to connect the hook to the rest of the tackle.

Line clip – small device incorporated into the spool of the reel to trap the line.

Livebait – live fish used as hookbait.

Lobworms – worm found in short grass – can be used as hookbait.

Loosefeed – particles or samples of bait deposited in the swim.

Lure – artificial bait, often resembling a fish.

- M -

Maggot – larvae of a fly – can be used as hookbait or loosefeed.

Maggot feeder – feeder with holes, used to feed maggots into the swim.

Mainline – line from the reel.

Margin – the edge of the swim close to the bank. Often a shelter for fish and a haven for fighting fish.

Match fishing – competitive form of coarse fishing.

Match rod – rod designed to be very strong but light and versatile.

Method (The) – variation on feeder fishing, where the hookbait is embedded into the feed.

Method feeder – feeder designed and used for fishing The Method.

Micro shot – very small split shot.

Monofilament – flexible and easy to use, low-cost fishing line.

- O -

Olivette – small cylindrical lead weight used on float rigs.

On the drop – fishing a float rig that sinks slowly into the water to catch the fish feeding high in the water.

- P -

Palomar – simple knot used to tie eyed hooks.

Particle bait – natural baits such as nuts, beans, peas, and cereals – can be used as hookbait or loosefeed.

Peg – pre-defined place for fishing directly in front of a swim.

Pellet – cylindrical bait, manufactured in various sizes, colours and flavours – can be used as hookbait or loosefeed.

Perch – stripy green fish with spines.

Permit – permission to fish in a certain place. Can be in the form of annual membership, or a day ticket, for example.

Pet food – dry or pasty food normally fed to dogs and cats – can be used as hookbait or loosefeed.

Pike – long cylindrical predator fish.

Pinkie – small larva of a fly – can be used as hookbait or loosefeed.

Platform – stable and transportable place from where to fish, incorporates a seat box and other equipment.

Plumb – to check the depth of the water using a float and a weight.

Plummet – weight used to the plumb.

Pole – long (8-14m) lightweight equipment used to get the float and tackle to the swim – like a rod.

Pole feeder pot – cup that clips onto the tip of a pole to transport loosefeed or groundbait to the swim.

Pole roller – device that provides a stable place for the pole to roll back on.

Pole winder – plastic winders designed to hold and protect pole float rigs.

Pole winder anchor – soft silicone rubber device, used to hold the loose end of a rig on a pole winder.

Pop-Up – buoyant boilie which floats off the lake bed.

Pre-baiting – introducing groundbait into the swim you intend to fish soon.

PTFE bush – plastic protector, used on the tip of poles – provides low friction with the elastic.

PVA – water soluble plastic.

PVA bag – bag designed to be filled with feed and tied to a rig.

PVA string – string designed to tie boilies or pellets to a rig.

- Q -

Quiver tip – rod with a very sensitive tip that moves when a fish bites.

- R -

Redworms – red worm found in compost heaps – can be used as hookbait.

Reel – device for holding the line and controlling the bait and the fish.

Riddle – mesh sieve used to separate maggots from the material they were grown in.

Rig – tackle comprising hook (or hooklength), mainline and a float, lead or feeder.

Rig bin – small plastic bin used for storing rigs without the risk of them being tangled.

Roach – silver fish with red fins, found in rivers and stillwaters.

Rod – long (3-5m) equipment (comprising a lightweight cylindrical tube with guides and handle) used to get the tackle to the swim.

Rod pod – device to fish two or three rods, side by side, at the same time.

Rod rest – device to hold a rod.

Rudd – silver fish with red fins, found in rivers and stillwaters.

Ruffe – small spiny fish, often found in stillwaters.

Running rig – leger rig where the weight is not directly attached to the hook. Can be used in rivers and stillwaters.

- S -

Scale – thin, flat shiny plates covering most fish.

Scales – device for weighing.

Scale count – the number of scales along the lateral line of a fish. Often used in fish identification.

Seat box – tackle box which can be used as a seat.

Session – time you spend fishing.

Shirt button – pattern of regularly spaced shot on a float rig.

Silver Bream – deep bodied silver fish, lives in slow-moving rivers and stillwaters.

Shot – small metallic spheres with a cut or split – used to add weight to a rig.

Short line – short piece of line between the pole float and the pole tip – useful in very windy conditions.

Shotting pattern – pattern of shot on the line below the float to suit the conditions.

Silicone rubber – tubing made of silicone rubber.

Skid bung – used to protect the ends of pole sections.

Slab – a Bream.

Slider – one way to float fish in deep water.

Slug – mollusc which can be used as hookbait.

Spade end hook – hook with a flattened piece of metal instead of an eye.

TERMINOLOGY

Specimen – any fish that is big for its species.

Spinning – method of fishing using a lure.

Split shot – shot.

Spod – rocket-shaped plastic tube filled with loosefeed and cast out into the swim – empties on impact with the water.

Spodding – using a spod.

Squat – tiny larva of a fly – can be used as hookbait or loosefeed.

Stalking – walking along a venue to spot fish and then trying to catch them.

Station – system that combines many pieces of equipment into the one unit, i.e. seat box, platform, bait boxes, etc.

Stick float – float with a bulbous section at the top, commonly used in rivers.

Stonfo adaptor – device used to connect the elastic at the tip of a pole to the line of a pole float rig.

Strike – action to hook the fish by lifting the rod and tightening the line.

Styl – variation on split shot in the form of a thin lead bar.

Surface fishing – fishing with floating baits to target fish feeding on the surface.

Swim – area of water you are fishing.

Swing tip rod – rod with a flexible tip attached by a piece of rubber tube.

Swivel – barrel with a freely rotating ring at each end. Used as a joint between the mainline and rig to reduce line twist.

- T -

Tackle – general term used for any fishing equipment.

Tackle box – box to store and carry smaller items of tackle.

Telescopic – rods or poles made of many sections that slide and fit together.

Tench – rounded olive coloured fish, mainly found in slow moving or still water.

Test curve – time and weight needed to make the rod tip bend 90 degrees from the rod butt.

Top section – top two, three or four sections of a pole, which are usually elasticated.

Total shot capacity – weight needed to set the float, so only the tip is showing.

Trolley – wheeled equipment used to get the tackle to the swim.

Trotting – method used when fishing a river with a stick float – to keep the bait moving with the flow.

- U -

Umbrella – protection from rain, wind and sunshine. Some have a fabric cover to make a quick and cheap form of bivvy.

Unhooking mat – padded waterproof sheet which protects the fish during unhooking.

- V -

Venue – place (lake, river, canal) you are fishing.

- W -

Waggler – straight-bodied float mainly used in still water – can have a bulbous bottom.

Watercraft – knowledge of fish and the environment they live in.

Weir – man-made water feature used to alter the flow characteristics of a river – often creating a large pool above the weir and fast-flowing water below the weir.

Wels Catfish – large dark scale-less predator fish.

Whip – short pole, mainly used for small fish.

Wide gape hook – hooks with greater distance between the hook point and the shank.

Wire trace – hooklength or section of line made from wire – used to prevent predators biting through the line.

Worm – small thin cylindrical creature, often found in soil or compost – can be used as hookbait.

- Z -

Zander – grey-brown predator fish with stripes, spines, and teeth.

GOING FISHING

Index

action, 28, 30
anti-reverse, 84
Artificial Baits, 52
attractant, 53
bail arm, 31, 83
bait, 20
Bait, 45, 79
Bait box, 44
bait boxes, 27
bank, 24, 25, 64
Bankstick, 42
banksticks, 43
barb, 38
Barbel, 15, 71
barbless, 38
Barbless, 39
Berries, 51
BITE, 99
Bite alarm, 43
Bleak, 8
Blockend, 37
bloodworms, 48
boats, 62

Boilies, 20, 52
Bowl, 45
braided, 32
brandlings, 47
Bread, 20, 48
Bread crust, 48
Bread flake, 48
Bread paste, 49
breaking strain, 79
Bream, 14
bridges, 62
Brollies, 26
brolly, 26
bulk shot, 93
butt, 43, 94
Cage feeder, 37
Canal, 18
Canals, 61
carp, 37
Carp, 17, 72
casters, 47
Casting, 93
catapult, 98

Catapult, 40
centrepin, 30
channel, 62
chinagraph pencil, 63, 66
Chinagraph pencil, 40
Chopped worms, 48
chub, 28
Chub, 13
Clothing, 25
Compleat Angler, 3
corn, 50
Corn, 20
Coshida, 51
Crucian Carp, 11
Dace, 9
Deadbait, 53
Deadbaits, 20
depth, 87
Disgorger, 39
disgorgers, 27
drag, 31
Drain, 18
Drains, 69
drink, 25
Drop-shotting, 75
Eel, 13
elastic, 29, 103
eye, 38
Fast moving rivers, 67
feeder, 85
Feeder, 19, 36
feeder rod, 29
fixed spool, 30
fixed spool reel, 31
float, 33, 83
Float, 19, 32
float rod, 28

Float stop, 40
Float Weights, 35
floats, 27
fluorocarbon, 32
Food, 25
gozzers, 46
gravel pits, 64
Grayling, 10
Groundbait, 53
Gudgeon, 8
Hemp, 50
Holdall, 44
Hook, 19, 38
hooklength, 32
hooks, 27
Isaac Walton, 3
Keepnet, 41
Knots, 55
Lake, 18
Lakes, 64
Landing net, 41
Larvae, 46
lead shot, 35
Leger, 19
Leger weights, 36
Length Conversion, 109
Licence, 23
line, 27
Line, 19, 32
Livebait, 53
lobworms, 47
Loosefeed, 54
Loosefeeding, 98
Lure, 19
Maggot, 20
Maggot feeder, 37
Maggots, 46

INDEX

Match Rod, 29
Meat, 51
Method feeder, 37
Molluscs, 51
monofilament, 32
nets, 27
Particle bait, 50
Pellets, 50
Pepperami, 51
Perch, 12, 28
permit, 23
Permit, 78
Pet food, 51
Pike, 16, 72
Pinkies, 46
plumbing, 39
Plummet, 39
pole, 27
Pole, 29, 84, 89
Pole float, 34
Pole roller, 43
Punched bread, 49
Pupae, 47
PVA bag, 37
quarries, 64
reel, 27
Reel, 30
reservoirs, 64
Rig, 31
Rigs, 79
river, 93
River, 18
Roach, 11
rod, 27
Rod, 28, 87

Rod rest, 43
rod rests, 27
Rudd, 12
Ruffe, 9
Seat, 26
Shelter, 26
shot, 35, 89
Silver Bream, 10
Slow-moving rivers, 65
slugs, 51
spade end, 38
Spinning, 73
split shot, 35
Squats, 46
SSG, 35
Stick float, 34
Strike, 100
sweetcorn, 50
Tackle, 27, 78
Tackle box, 41
Tackle Box, 79
Tench, 14
Trolley, 44
Trotting, 93
umbrella, 26
Unhooking mat, 45
Waggler, 34
Weather, 77
Weight, 35
Weight Conversion, 107
weights, 27
weir pool, 67
Wels Catfish, 16, 72
Worms, 47
Zander, 15, 72

Printed in Great Britain
by Amazon